T H E
Zen
of Cooking

THE Zen of Cooking

CREATIVE COOKING WITH AND WITHOUT RECIPES

Lucille Naimer

THE OVERLOOK PRESS
WOODSTOCK • NEW YORK

First published in 1995 by
The Overlook Press
Lewis Hollow Road
Woodstock, New York 12498

Library of Congress Cataloging-in-Publication Data
Naimer, Lucille.
    The zen of cooking : how recipes can teach us to cook without them , Lucille Naimer
    p. cm.
    1. Cookery. I. Naimer, Lucille. II. Title.
TX714.H95   1995
641.5 – dc20   94-47244
                                                                     CIP

Book design by Bernard Schleifer
Typeset by AeroType, Inc.
Manufactured in the United States of America
ISBN: 0-87951-594-5
First Printing

"Flow with whatever may happen and let your mind be free.
Stay centered by accepting whatever you are doing. This is the ultimate."
CHUANG TZU

"Enjoyment is not a goal.
It is a feeling that accompanies important ongoing activity."
PAUL GOODMAN

CONTENTS

BREAKING THE THYME BARRIER

RAM DAS: "How will I know God?"
TEACHER: "Feed people."
RAM DAS: "How will I become enlightened?"
TEACHER: "Serve them."

LUCILLE IS SITTING ON A STOOL BY A COUNTER THAT SEPARATES THE KITCHEN from the dining room. She is writing the introduction to *The Zen of Cooking*. Claire, her sister, is in the kitchen, having decided to cook a peanut butter pasta. She is gathering together all the pots, pans, and utensils she'll need for the meal.

Lucille looks up from her paper, momentarily distracted by the noise, but then returns to her writing task: *What you are about to read is a book using Zen philosophy to help teach us to cook without recipes. We have been programmed to feel that a recipe is needed to create a "gourmet" meal. We have been conditioned to think that cookbooks make the rules. With these beliefs we give up our innate creative and intuitive abilities of self-expression through cooking.*

Distracted again by the opening and closing of a cupboard door, she notices that Claire has taken out a jar of peanut butter. "I hope you're using the crunchy this time," she says. Claire, raising her eyebrow, says, "No, I like the creamy."

Lucille sighs and refocuses on her writing: *The book's objective is to "slice" through this programming by introducing the reader to a style of cooking that does not depend on recipes. By providing new ways of experiencing all areas related to food, the creative process is re-established. This does not mean, "throw out the cookbooks." Rather, in keeping with the Zen philosophy of becoming one's own teacher, it is to show how cookbooks and recipes can be used as tools in this method without becoming the absolute authorities.*

It also explores ingredients, spices, and condiments as the palette for the cook; and with a few "rules and tools" of how to "mix the colors," we are on our way to cooking without recipes.

Smiling at having satisfactorily completed this thought, she looks across the counter and reads this part to Claire. After it meets with her sister's approval, Lucille says, "How about sliced, candied ginger mixed in with the peanut butter?" Claire, at first wary, begins to like the thought. "You know that actually sounds interesting. I'll try a little bit of it and see how it works. But hand me the sesame oil. It definitely needs some more of that."

Lucille returns to her writing: *What has prompted the writing of this book is the response of friends and family to our cooking. It has "blown them away" to discover that recipes have not been used. And so there have always been an array of questions as to how this was all accomplished. The Zen of Cooking attempts to answer such questions in a manner that can lead others to personal expression through cooking while having fun times in the kitchen. Imagine the satisfaction you will feel when someone, enjoying your delicious meal, asks, "That was the greatest! Where did you get the recipe?" And you reply, "It's my own creation."*

Reading aloud the conclusion to the introduction, Lucille gets up from the stool, picks up a jar of hot pepper flakes and surreptitiously edges towards the saucepan. Claire, on guard for just such an assault, suddenly turns around and faces her sister: "Oh no you don't! What were those words you just wrote in the introduction? 'It's my own creation.' I'll put flakes in *my* creation if and when I want to, thank you!"

Lucille, meekly handing her the jar, "Okay, okay. I'll be especially good. But next thyme try the flakes. It'll work."

THE Zen of Cooking

COOKING AND CREATIVITY

*"When you do something, you should burn yourself completely, like
a good bonfire, leaving no trace of yourself."*
—SHUNRYU SUZUKI

THE ZEN MASTERS HAVE A TERM FOR THE ZEN EXPERIENCE. IT IS "SATORI," THE
moment of awakening when we embrace life and are at one with
whatever we are doing. It is spontaneity; it is no-conflict. It is the
moment when everything clicks. It is sensational.

The Zen experience of satori can be attained in countless ways;
often it comes as one loses oneself in a creative activity. One of our
goals in writing this book is to help the reader as he or she seeks this
transcendent experience through cooking. Another, more modern
word to explain this transcendent state is "flow." For his book, *Flow:
The Psychology of Optimal Experience* (Harper Perennial, 1980), Dr. Mihaly
Csikszentmihalhi, a professor of psychology at the University of Chi-
cago, studied artists to learn what put them in a state of creative "flow,"
which he defines as a state in which one loses sense of anything
outside the activity in which one is engaged. What he learned is that it
is challenge, stretching beyond what one has previously accomplished,
that can transform a routine activity into a flow, or satori, experience.
Flow is a state of optimal performance, creativity, and enjoyment that
can be attained only by pushing beyond what one has previously
accomplished in a given field of endeavor.

This book itself represents this paradoxical nature of the satori
experience: that both mastery and challenge that takes us beyond our

previous level of mastery is required for satori to occur. This book is about cooking without recipes, yet it presents dozens of them and suggests dozens more, reconciling a basic contradiction between the West's emphasis on a "how to" instructional approach to life's tasks and the East's just being there attitude. It is about learning the rules and then breaking them, or at least turning them upside down.

The ultimate aim of *The Zen of Cooking* is to stimulate creativity, to put you in a state of flow in the kitchen so you will cook better, more inventively, and with more self-assurance and enjoyment than you ever thought possible.

Hoping that Claire is lost in thought searching the refrigerator for additional ingredients to put into her stew simmering on the stove, Lucille furtively removes a bottle of dried sage from the cabinet and heads towards the stove.

Claire glances up from the refrigerator to ask: "When are you going to get to The Zen Six-Steps?"

Lucille replies, "Uh. Right now," as she covertly slips the sage into her pocket, returns to the table, and picks up her pen.

The Zen of Cooking addresses the tension between the tenets of "being there" and of "how to" by recognizing the importance of both. Zen speaks of enlightenment through an introspection that has no doctrine, no prescribed patterns, rules, or recipes by which the beckoner can mold the external world. Western cookbooks tell us "repeat this, repeat that" and all will turn out well in the end. Zen points its followers towards their own resources and, therefore, their own unique relationship to the universe. Cookbooks tell us "use this, use that" and yours will taste just like Mama's old-fashioned apple pie. Each approach knows success and failure. By synthesizing the two, *The Zen of Cooking* creates a new set of successes and failures.

When satori is experienced, patterns appear that document the creative process. In the field of cooking these patterns are called recipes. *The Zen of Cooking,* in the best of Western intentions at active inventiveness, attempts to use old recipes to create new recipes and new recipes to transform old recipes into something new.

If this seems too abstract, bake a batch of buns. They seem perfect—taste, texture, and smell. You paid close attention to each detail. A week later you recreate the same conditions except that is

---

impossible, isn't it? At the very least it is a week later, making the time factor different. Since the senses of taste, texture, and smell are relative to what was experienced before, this factor cannot be duplicated either because you have already experienced perfection.

And there are other more subtle factors that cannot be duplicated. Paying close attention originally may have meant unconscious mistakes were made that contributed to the perfect batch; but no amount of concentration could replicate these same unknown errors. Even the barometer readings may be different. And, of course, ambiance cannot be objectified. Perhaps that is why subsequent batches, for better or worse, never seem quite the same. Perhaps, had you remained momentarily still, you would have noticed that the creative significance was to be found in the color of the first batch rather than the taste, texture, or smell. Perhaps the problem was in the effort at re-creation when it should have been directed towards a new creation.

There are steps to understanding as they apply to the Zen experience in general and *The Zen of Cooking* in particular. Learn them, practice them, ponder them, discard them, and above all, enjoy the sensorial experience of creation through cooking.

THE ZEN SIX STEPS TO CREATIVE COOKING

Step One: *"Zen aims at freedom, but its practice is disciplined."*
—GARY SNYDER

This first step encompasses the paradox we mentioned above: that to get into the flow of cooking creatively, one must achieve a level of mastery and then reach beyond that level so that the activity is a challenge. What is mastery and what is a challenge will be different for every cook; what is the same is that sense of striving, of reaching beyond what we've already accomplished in the kitchen to reach new culinary heights. Don't make the same old salad for dinner every night. Go beyond that salad, which you have already mastered, and try something new.

Step Two: *"Teachers open the door, but you must enter by yourself."*
—CHINESE PROVERB

Don't depend on cooking classes and cookbooks as the only sources of your creative expression. You say you want to prepare a salad to go with dinner? And you also say you have a taste for oranges? Use that as a starting point and build on it. But don't go to the cookbook; look within. Trust your instincts and follow your gastronomic bliss, using what you have learned from your own cooking experiences and from cookbooks in the past, but moving beyond these teachers to a new realm.

Step Three: *"Zen is to have the heart and soul of a little child."*
—TAKUAN

Children approach all activities with a sense of fun and playfulness. This approach is what we aim to duplicate as creative cooks. Children also have little sense of limitations—for them, everything is possible. So, approach cooking with the audacity of a child; say to yourself, "Go ahead, I dare you. Try that strange-sounding combination of oranges and raw onions in a salad and see what results."

Step Four: *"Knowledge is knowing as little as possible."*
—CHARLES BUKOWSKI

Unlearn that which you have learned, that which has become habit and rote. Look right rather than left, and perhaps you'll be on to what sounds like a promising combination of oranges, cucumbers, mangoes, and sweet Vidalia onions in that salad.

Step Five: *"Life is not a problem to be solved but a reality to experience."*
—KIERKEGAARD

Don't be discouraged by what appears to be a negative result. There are no wrong answers. What may at first look like a deadend or a failure may provide an opportunity to enter into and experience previously unknown territories of cooking. In the Zen of cooking, each experience is an essential stepping stone along the continuum of the creative process. The concept of a mistake does not exist. How else could one account for the delectable and refreshing taste of an orange, cucumber, mango, sweet onion salad with tangy mint dressing had not the grimace at the idea of oranges and raw onions first been experienced.

Step Six: *"God is in the details."*
—MIES VAN DER ROHE

"Details are all there are."
—MAEZUMI

Attention to the details keeps the cook aware of sensorial data, the basis of creative cooking. Does it look right? Does it feel right? Does it sound right? Does it have the right aroma? Does it taste right? If the answer to any of these questions is "no," then the creative cook can fine-tune the dish until everything is just right, that is to say, just the way he or she wants it to be at that moment. Does that salad, which looks beautiful, feels crunchy, sounds crisp, smells minty, sweet, and tart need anything else? How about a sprinkling of slightly salty sunflower seeds? Now it tastes like perfection!

HOW RECIPES CAN TEACH US TO COOK WITHOUT THEM

"Imagination is more important than knowledge."
— ALBERT EINSTEIN

RECIPES CAN BE DECEIVING. IT MAY APPEAR THAT RECIPES HAVE NOTHING more to offer than a step-by-step procedure for combining and cooking a list of ingredients into a finished product. But for the creative cook who brings to every task the search for the essence of life, valuable discoveries can be made in examining the more subliminal nature of recipes.

It was on one of these examinations that a difference emerged between *core* ingredients—those necessary for a specific type of food—and *elective* ingredients—those offering the food varying taste sensations. The significance of this can be illustrated by using the following four baking recipes to get a clear image of the core ingredients. The electives will be covered later on in this chapter.

UNCOVERING THE "CORE"

OATMEAL CHIP BROWNIES

6 to 8 large brownies

2	*ounces unsweetened baking chocolate*
*½	*cup unsweetened butter*
*4	*tablespoons Hershey's chocolate syrup*
1	*cup Old Fashioned Quaker Oats*
¼	*teaspoon salt*
*2	*teaspoons baking powder*
*2	*eggs or 1 egg and 1 egg white*
2	*teaspoons vanilla*
8	*ounces semisweet chocolate chips*

Preheat the oven to 350°.

Grease an 11 × 7-inch baking dish. Melt the unsweetened chocolate and the butter over very low heat, stirring until the chocolate and butter are completely melted. Stir in the Hershey's syrup. Set aside on the counter to cool.

Grind the oats in a food processor or coffee grinder to medium-coarse consistency. In a small bowl stir together the oats, salt, and baking powder. Pour the chocolate mixture into a large bowl. Using a whisk or an electric hand beater, beat in the eggs and blend well. Add the vanilla. Blend in the oatmeal mixture a little at a time. If the batter becomes too thick, add a little water. Blend well. Stir in the chocolate chips. Pour the batter into a greased pan. Bake 20 minutes at 350°. Do not overcook.

*Core ingredients.

BANANA NUT CARROT CAKE SQUARES

8 to 10 servings

*2 cups unbleached flour
 1 teaspoon salt
 1 tablespoon ground cinnamon
 1 tablespoon ground cloves
*3 teaspoons baking powder
*3 large eggs
 ½ cup brown sugar
*½ cup honey
*¾ cup vegetable oil
*½ cup orange, pineapple, or apple juice
 1 cup grated carrots
 1 cup mashed ripe bananas
 1 cup chopped walnuts

Preheat the oven to 350°. Grease a 9 × 12-inch baking dish. In a large bowl, sift together the flour, salt, cinnamon, cloves, and baking powder. In a smaller bowl, beat together the eggs, add sugar, honey, and whisk in the oil and juice. Mix into the dry ingredients. Stir in the carrots, bananas, and walnuts. Pour mixture into the baking dish. Bake 40 to 45 minutes or until an inserted toothpick in the center comes out clean. Cool 50 to 60 minutes. Serve with vanilla yogurt or ice cream.

---

*Core ingredients.

PUMPKIN SPICE SQUARES

approximately 9 squares

*1½	cups cooked pumpkin (or use canned pumpkin)
*1½	cups bleached flour
2	teaspoons cinnamon
2	teaspoons ground allspice
½	teaspoon salt
*1	teaspoon baking soda
*1	stick unsalted butter—softened
½	cup sugar
*2	eggs
2	tablespoons grated lemon peel
2	teaspoons vanilla
*½	cup water

Preheat the oven to 350°. In a small bowl, combine the flour, cinnamon, allspice, salt, and baking soda. In a mixing bowl, beat by hand the butter and sugar together. Beat until fluffy. Add the eggs and pumpkin and blend well. Beat in the lemon peel, vanilla, and water. Pour into the flour mixture a little at a time. Blend well. Pour mixture into a greased 11 × 7-inch pan. Bake 25 to 30 minutes or until a toothpick inserted in the center comes out clean. Cool before cutting into squares.

*Core ingredients.

WHOLE WHEAT PEANUT BUTTER COOKIES

approximately 2 dozen cookies

*1   egg
½   cup brown sugar
¼   cup sugar
*½   cup butter
½   cup creamy peanut butter
*2   teaspoons vanilla
*1½ cups whole wheat flour
1   teaspoon salt
*½   teaspoon baking soda
1   cup peanuts (not raw)

In a mixing bowl, beat the egg, sugars, and butter until fluffy. Add the peanut butter and mix again. Stir in the vanilla. In another bowl, mix the whole wheat flour, salt, and baking soda. Stir the flour mixture into the peanut butter mixture. Stir in the peanuts. Chill in the refrigerator for at least 1 hour.

Preheat the oven to 350°. Drop small spoonfuls of the mixture on to an ungreased cookie sheet (preferably nonstick) and bake 10 to 15 minutes.

> TEACHER: "What is an egg?"
> STUDENT: "An egg is an unhatched chicken."
> TEACHER: "No, an egg is a binder."

The above recipes have in common the following core ingredients which are essential for the baking process.

---

*Core ingredients.

- *Eggs* are the *binder* that holds all the ingredients together.
- *Baking powder* or *baking soda* produce *air bubbles* that allow for the leavening process so that the dough will rise.
- *Butter/oil* acts as the *lubricant* which permits the dough to rise smoothly, adding moisture throughout.
- *Flour* gives the dough its *substance*.
- *Liquid* is necessary for the mixture to combine into one basic substance. Purees, yogurt, applesauce, honey, and syrups fall into this category.

These are the core ingredients needed to lay the groundwork for most baking recipes. (In cooking there are always exceptions.) This is an important piece of information because when you wish to bake a cake, you no longer have to consult a recipe for its core ingredients. Consider the core a blank canvas on which you will paint (without numbers) your own cake creation.

But where's the beauty, the flair, the excitement in a blank canvas without the paint? It is in the selection and use of the electives that the cook's personal touch emerges and in which the cook's unique personality finds expression.

DISCOVERING THE ELECTIVES

Looking back at the Banana Nut Carrot Cake Squares recipe on page 9, we can see that the items not asterisked are the electives: walnuts, brown sugar, bananas, salt, carrots, cinnamon, and cloves. How do you feel about these ingredients for the taste of the cake? Perhaps there are others you would add to improve the flavor or some you would eliminate. Look at the electives in the other recipes and maybe they will stimulate your palate. I might add some nutmeg, some dried fruit, or perhaps use crushed pineapple instead of bananas.

The following pie crust recipes will illustrate the importance of electives and their relationship to the core ingredients.

SWEET OATBRAN PIE CRUST

1	cup unbleached flour
½	teaspoon salt
*1	tablespoon oatbran
¼	cup canola oil
2	tablespoons cold milk
*2	tablespoons sugar

Sift the flour into a bowl and add the salt, oil, and milk. Mix with a fork into a dough. Gather the dough in your hands to form a ball. Refrigerate 1 hour. Roll the dough between two pieces of wax paper to fit an 8-inch pie pan. Peel off the top piece of wax paper and turn pastry side down into the pie pan. Remove the second piece of wax paper and fit the pastry into the pan, trim and decorate the edges.

Preheat the oven to 450° and bake the pie shell at 350° for about 15 minutes or until set and lightly browned.

NUTTY PIE CRUST

2	tablespoons sugar
1	cup unbleached flour
1	teaspoon salt
6 to 7	tablespoons cold water
½	cup unsalted butter well-chilled
*½	cup ground almonds

*Elective ingredients.

Using a food processor, combine the almonds, sugar, flour, and salt. Cut the butter into ½-inch pats and add to flour mixture. Process until clumps are formed. Add water, a small amount at a time, until the ingredients form a dough-like consistency. Remove and shape into a ball. Wrap the dough in wax paper or plastic wrap and chill for at least 1 hour.

If you do not have a food processor, mix the sugar, flour, and salt in a large bowl. Then cut the butter into small pieces, and with two knives or a fork or just with your fingers, blend the butter into the flour until the flour feels like cornmeal. Gather the dough into a ball. Wrap and refrigerate for one hour. After refrigerated, roll dough between two pieces of wax paper to fit a 9-inch pan. Peel off the top piece of wax paper and turn pastry side down into the pie pan. Remove the second piece of wax paper and press the pastry dough into the pan. Trim and decorate the edges.

CURRY PIE CRUST FOR QUICHE

1   *cup whole wheat pastry flour*
1   *cup unbleached white flour*
*3   *teaspoons curry powder*
8   *ounces cream cheese, cut into quarters*
3 to 6   *tablespoons ice water*

Blend the whole wheat, white flour, and curry powder in a food processor for 8 seconds. Add cream cheese quarters one at a time until blended. Add water slowly until dough consistency forms. Wrap the dough in wax paper or plastic wrap. Refrigerate for 1 hour. After refrigerated, roll dough between two pieces of wax paper to fit a 9-inch pan. Peel off the top piece of wax paper and turn pastry side down into the pie pan. Remove the second piece of wax paper and press the pastry dough into the pan. Trim and decorate.

---

*Elective ingredients.

Once again we can see a theme running throughout all these recipes. The core consists of some kind of flour and/or related flour product, butter and/or related butter product (oil, margarine, lard, cream cheese), and liquid. All additional ingredients therefore must be elective by elimination. In the Sweet Oatbran Pie Crust, the oatbran and sugar are the electives. In the Nutty Pie Crust, the nuts and sugar are the electives. And obviously the curry in the Curry Pie Crust is the elective. If you can use oatbran, then why not any grain? If you can use nuts, then why not anything pulverized (graham crackers, Oreos, or any other kind of nut)? The curry as an elective opens up more possibilities for flavors—garlic, rosemary, basil, chili spice. We rarely have to do the same crust twice.

Looking back at the Whole Wheat Peanut Butter Cookies recipe on page 11, we see that the electives include 1 cup of peanuts. Perhaps walnuts or pignoli nuts or a combination could be substituted. If the recipe calls for vanilla, why not try powdered ginger or cinnamon? Instead of nuts, one could use 1 cup of semisweet chocolate bits or even add flaked coconut (1 cup). And if you like raisins, 1 cup of these instead of peanuts or ½ cup raisins and ½ cup nuts could taste just great!

The information provided by examining the baking and pie crust recipes reveals that a recipe can be divided into its core and elective ingredients and each part enhances the other: the former is given vitality, the latter substance. Once having made this discovery, the creative imagination of the cook can stimulate a world of possibilities—not only in its application to baking but to all other areas of cooking as well. The list is (z)endless.

USING COOKBOOKS AS INSPIRATION

"Do not seek to follow in the footsteps of the wise. Seek what they sought."

—BASHO

SINCE THE CREATION OF THE FIRST RECIPE, COOKBOOKS HAVE DOCUMENTED THE meandering history of the culinary arts and its sometimes paradoxical movement towards ever-expanding nuances of palatable tastes. Cookbooks can be used to stimulate the senses and inspire the creative cook.

The word "paradoxical" was chosen with care. As in virtually every other human endeavor, there are times when the world at large seems ready and open for new possibilities and other times when the aperture of opportunity seems to close completely. But in the Zen tradition of the paradoxical, what appears to be the desolation and barrenness of one era can turn out to be the mother of the next era's inventiveness. How else can one explain the emergence of current culinary creativity out of the apparent barrenness of the Levittown kitchens in the 1950s? How else can one explain the movement from overly-cooked frozen beans and Spam-in-the-can to freshly picked basil from the vegetable garden in the cook's backyard?

This chapter illustrates how to examine cookbooks of great chefs, cookbooks from around the world, and specialty cookbooks, in order to move beyond the recipe and into the creative flow of cooking without recipes. The cookbook of a great chef can be compared to the work of a great painter, the poems of a poet, the pots made by a potter, the novels of a writer. Each presents a unique style, a particular creative statement. If Picasso and Van Gogh were to paint the same still life, two completely different representations and easily distinguishable styles would result. Part of this creativity was the outcome of many years of experimentation with the styles and schools of their contemporaries and predecessors.

The recipes of a great chef also reflect this same development. One or two recipes will not necessarily reveal it, but when reading an entire cookbook of recipes, the style begins to unfold, and its discovery is as exciting as uncovering the major plot of a novel. An ingredient from here, a sauce from there, a spice from who knows where, and suddenly the theme is revealed, the chef's style indelibly imprinted on the reader's mind. When this clicks there is something new to work with and a further step taken on the creative path.

Wolfgang Puck is the perfect example of a contemporary chef whose original style emanates throughout his recipes: a fusion of processes and ingredients from French, Chinese, and Japanese cuisines, combined with a California emphasis on fresh and unusual fruits and vegetables, and cooked with a minimal amount of fat. By his use of special crusts and unique choice of toppings (e.g., smoked salmon and shrimp), he has even turned pizza into a gourmet offering. His creative eclecticism is illustrated in the following three recipes from *The Wolfgang Puck Cookbook: Recipes from Spago, Chinois, and Points East and West:* Lobster with Sweet Ginger, Artichoke Mousse, and Szechuan Beef.

LOBSTER WITH SWEET GINGER

serves 2

1 *piece fresh ginger, approximately 1 inch*
2 *cloves garlic, minced*
¾ *cup plum wine or port*
2 *tablespoons rice wine vinegar*
1 *2-pound lobster, split lengthwise*
2 *tablespoons peanut oil*
2 *tablespoons unsalted butter*
4 *scallions, cut into ⅜-inch slices*
1 to 2 *teaspoons curry powder*
¼ *cup dry white wine*
½ *cup fish stock (see below)*
½ *teaspoon dried hot chili flakes*
1 *tablespoon Chinese black vinegar or balsamic vinegar*
½ *cup heavy cream*
   salt
   freshly ground pepper

1. Preheat the oven to 500°.

2. Peel the ginger, reserving the peels, and cut it into fine julienne strips. Cut the peels into coarse julienne strips and set aside.

3. In a small saucepan, cook the ginger and garlic with ½ cup of the plum wine and the rice wine vinegar until 1 tablespoon of liquid remains. Remove from the heat and reserve.

4. Place a heavy heat-proof 12-inch skillet over high heat until it is very hot. Add the oil and heat it almost to the smoking point. Carefully add the lobster halves, meat side down. Cook 3 minutes. Turn the lobster over and add 1 tablespoon of the butter. Continue to sauté

until the lobster is just cooked. Remove the lobster from the skillet and keep warm.

5. Add the scallions, ginger peels, and curry powder to the skillet. (Be careful, the handle might be hot.) Sauté the mixture lightly for 10 to 15 seconds, then whisk in the remaining plum wine and the white wine, stock, chili flakes, and vinegar. Reduce the liquid to ½ cup. Add the cream and reduce it by half. Add any liquid from the julienne of ginger, then whisk in the remaining tablespoon of butter. Season the sauce to taste with salt and pepper.

6. Crack the lobster claws with the back of a large chef's knife.

PRESENTATION: Arrange the lobster halves on a warm oval platter, meat side up. Strain the sauce over the lobster, then sprinkle the sweet ginger on top. Garnish with Fried Baby Spinach Leaves.

FISH STOCK (MAKES 1 QUART)

2   pounds fish skeletons, cut into pieces
2   tablespoons vegetable or other flavorless oil
1   small carrot, peeled and sliced
½   onion, sliced
1   small celery, sliced
2   cups dry white wine
1   bouquet garni (a bundle of aromatic herbs, usually consisting of
     parsley, thyme, peppercorns, and a bay leaf tied together and used
     to flavor stocks, soups, stews, and sauces)
1   quart water, approximately

1. Clean the fish bones under cold running water, removing the gills from the head and any traces of blood on the frames.

*Use the skeletons of saltwater fish such as sole, John Dory, turbot, halibut, or other very fresh non-oily fish for stock.

2. In a large saucepan, heat the oil. In it sweat the fish bones and vegetables over low heat, covered, for 10 minutes, stirring once or twice to prevent them from browning.

3. Deglaze the pan with the wine, then add enough water to cover the bones and vegetables by 2 inches. Add the bouquet garni and bring the liquid to a boil. Skim the froth from the surface, reduce the heat, and simmer the stock for 20 to 25 minutes.

4. Strain the stock into a clean saucepan. Bring it to a boil and reduce it over moderate heat to 1 quart.

NOTE: Fish stock will keep in the refrigerator for 2 to 3 days or frozen for 2 to 3 weeks. After that time the flavor begins to fade.

FRIED BABY SPINACH LEAVES

Wash large spinach leaves, cut off the stems, and dry them well. Heat peanut oil to 375° and in it fry the spinach until crisp and translucent. Be careful not to get splattered! Remove the leaves to paper towels to drain, and salt them lightly (just like potato chips). The spinach should have a jade green color.

ARTICHOKE MOUSSE

serves 3 to 4

4 or 5	**very large artichokes**
2	**lemons, halved**
4	**tablespoons (2 ounces) unsalted butter, at room temperature**
about 2	**tablespoons heavy cream**
	salt
	freshly ground pepper

1. Trim away the leaves from the artichokes to expose the bottoms. Rub the cut surfaces with lemon to prevent oxidation.

2. Bring a large pot of salted water to a boil. Add the juice of ½ lemon and the artichoke bottoms, cover with a linen towel or several thicknesses of paper towels, and cook until the artichokes are tender, 40 to 50 minutes.

3. Remove the artichokes and drain. Remove and discard the fiber from the center of the chokes.

4. Puree the artichoke bottoms in a food processor with the butter. Pass the puree through a tamis or fine strainer into a heavy saucepan and heat through. Stir in the cream and correct the seasonings with salt, pepper, and lemon juice.

PRESENTATION: Serve as a side dish to accompany lamb or chicken or use as a bed for sliced meats and poultry.

NOTE: To reheat, place the mousse in a heavy saucepan, add 1 tablespoon each of unsalted butter and heavy cream. Heat slowly, stirring constantly.

SZECHUAN BEEF

serves 4

GINGER VINAIGRETTE

- 1 small shallot, minced
- ½ inch piece fresh ginger, peeled and minced
- 1 small clove garlic, minced
- ⅓ cup light salad oil or extra-virgin olive oil
- 1 tablespoon dark sesame oil
- ¼ cup rice wine vinegar or 3 tablespoons Chinese black vinegar
  salt
  freshly ground pepper

SZECHUAN BEEF

- 4 well-trimmed New York steaks, 1½ inches thick
  light sesame oil
- 1 tablespoon Chinese or cracked black peppercorns
- 1 large shallot, chopped
- 1 cup dry red wine
- 1 cup Brown Veal Stock (see below)
- ½ teaspoon dried red chili flakes
- 1 large clove garlic, chopped
- ½ inch piece fresh ginger, peeled and chopped
- 4 tablespoons (2 ounces) unsalted butter
- 1 tablespoon mushroom soy or other soy sauce
- 2 tablespoons chopped fresh cilantro
  salt
- 2 bunches watercress, stemmed and cleaned
- 1 bunch spinach, smaller leaves only
- 2 green onions, thinly sliced, for garnish

1. Prepare the vinaigrette: mix all the vinaigrette ingredients together. Taste and correct the seasonings.

2. Prepare the beef: drizzle the steaks with sesame oil and pat them with Chinese or black peppercorns on both sides. Place on a dish, cover with plastic wrap, refrigerate, and let marinate several hours or overnight.

3. Place the shallot and red wine in a saucepan, bring to a boil and reduce by two-thirds. Add the stock, chili flakes, garlic, and ginger. Continue to reduce the sauce until it is thickened slightly. Whisk in the butter, a little at a time, over low heat (or on the side of the stove). Add the soy sauce and cilantro. (Mushroom soy sauce is less salty, darker, and thicker than regular soy sauce and is what we use at Chinois. It is available in Oriental markets. If you use regular soy sauce, add it slowly and taste frequently to prevent oversalting.) Correct the seasonings and keep the sauce warm.

4. Preheat a grill until hot. Remove the steaks from the marinade and salt each side lightly. Grill the steaks about 5 minutes on each side, until medium rare. If a charcoal or gas grill is not available to you, sauté the steaks in a little butter and sesame oil. Transfer the steaks to a cutting board and let them rest.

5. Toss the watercress and the smallest, tenderest of the spinach leaves with a little ginger vinaigrette. Divide among 4 dinner plates and set aside.

6. Cut each steak diagonally into ⅜-inch slices. If the meat has gotten too cool, reheat slightly in the sauce.

PRESENTATION: Overlap slices of steak down the center of each side. Reduce the sauce slightly if necessary and spoon it over the steak. Sprinkle green onions on top.

VARIATION: To make this a Southwestern dish, use extra-virgin olive oil in place of the sesame oil, omit the ginger, and use a small piece of jalapeño pepper in the sauce reduction.

BROWN VEAL STOCK
(MAKES ½ GALLON STOCK, OR 1 QUART DEMI-GLAZE)

10	pounds veal bones, cut into 2-inch pieces
2	onions, quartered
2	carrots, coarsely chopped
1	leek, coarsely chopped
2	tomatoes, quartered
2	bay leaves
1	teaspoon black peppercorns
2	sprigs thyme
1	head garlic, halved (optional)
1	gallon water

1. Preheat the oven to 450°.

2. Spread the bones and onions in a single layer in a large roasting pan and place in the oven. Turn the bones as they brown until they are a dark golden brown on all sides. Transfer the bones to a large stockpot. Add the vegetables, bay leaves, peppercorns, thyme, and garlic, if desired.

3. Pour off the fat from the roasting pan, then deglaze the pan with 2 cups of water, scraping up any particles sticking to the bottom of the pan. Add this liquid to the stockpot and pour in enough water to cover the bones by 2 inches. Bring the water to a boil, reduce the heat, and let the mixture simmer at least 6 hours and as long as 24 hours, skimming the foam and fat as necessary.

4. Strain the liquid through a sieve into a clean stockpot. Remove any last traces of foam or fat. Bring the stock to a boil and reduce it over low heat until the flavor is full-bodied. There should be about 1 gallon. To make veal demi-glace, reduce the stock by half.

5. Refrigerate the stock for 2 to 3 days or freeze it in small quantities. It will freeze well for 2 to 3 months. Demi-glace will keep up to 1 week in the refrigerator and in the freezer for 2 to 3 months.

NOTE: Veal stock can be used instead of brown duck stock or lamb stock. It has a neutral flavor.

In the first recipe the ginger, plum wine, rice wine vinegar, Chinese black vinegar, and hot chili flakes, commonly used ingredients of the Chinese cuisine, have been chosen for their pungent aroma and flavor. The fish stock and heavy cream, derived from the base ingredients of French sauces, will be combined with the Chinese flavor for a creative East meets West union.

The second recipe, the Artichoke Mousse, comes from the old French tradition of mousse making. This is to accompany any lamb or chicken dish, regardless of whether it is in a French, Chinese, or Southwestern style. Here again the imaginative combination of East and West.

When the Szechuan Beef, derived from the popular Chinese stir-fried dish of the Szechuan province, is incorporated into a salad with the addition of fresh greens (a Wolfgang Puck signature), the dish becomes an exotic mixture of California freshness and Chinese flavors.

The creative blend of such diverse and seemingly disparate cuisines is a sign of the times, of an era that could find no better representation than in the enthusiastic experimentations of Wolfgang Puck. There is of course his charisma: cooking is his medium—mystery and magic abound beyond that of a witch's brew. But there is no mystery in how he does it: he selects the finest and freshest ingredients, extracts them from global gardens and farms, and matches and prepares them from his knowledge of a wide variety of cuisines. And that is a culinary pattern we can cull from looking at his style. We can do with these basic, uncomplicated skills of selecting, extracting, matching, and preparing—perhaps not with his mastery but always producing our own mysteries.

"How fortunate we all are to be part of such an adventurous age. No longer fearing to cross boundaries, the cook goes into unexplored territory without intimidation. You don't need to be a Cordon Bleu graduate to do it. Think of cooking as an outlet for your ideas, a release for the artist in you. It took me nearly eight years to break away from the tradition of my European training and feel free to experiment with new ways. But you can start now. Your American heritage is a wonderful one. Let the world know you are proud of it!"

—WOLFGANG PUCK

COOKBOOKS FROM AROUND THE WORLD

About half the cookbooks written are devoted to international cuisine. While reading through recipes, let yourself be taken to a faraway land where the aroma of the ingredients can inspire new ways of cooking. And just as the many recipes of a chef reveal his style, it is important to examine not one but a variety of cookbooks from a regional/ethnic area to become familiar with that style of cooking.

We recently checked out two books on East Indian cooking, needing a quick brushup on techniques and some inspiration in this category. It was interesting to see how one author geared his recipes to the American way of cooking by giving ways to prepare roasts, whole fish, and large fowl. But East Indians rarely serve these. The second cookbook was in stark contrast, keeping to the more traditional East Indian approach of cutting up the meat, mixing it into other ingredients, and emphasizing the use of unusual spices. Even if the reader did not know which was traditional and which Western-oriented, the contrast would have caught the curious eye and if one simply followed curiosity around the corner, a third or fourth cookbook would have revealed the ethnic characteristics most commonly shared.

Ideas for new recipes started to emerge as we glanced through the first book. Instead of using the Indian spices for fowl, we used them in the stuffing and did a Chinese sweet-and-sour sauce to baste the bird. We also came up with a good curry salad dressing.

The second book, more detailed in the area of spices and preparations, inspired a curry pasta sauce with tandori roasted chicken.

By reading through cookbooks one finds certain methods and spices used repeatedly. This then becomes the extracted theme. Any Chinese cookbook with stir frying will give the basics: a wok and spoon, oil, a group of spices and condiments, and vegetables, meat, fish, chicken, usually dipped in egg white. This makes for a good foundation. We can get creative by using Mexican or East Indian spices with this Chinese base, and by serving it with pasta instead of rice.

Eventually all this will lead to a variety of different recipes extracted from the knowledge of spices and procedures in just a few hours of enjoyable study.

Specialty cookbooks explore in depth particular types of food (e.g., vegetables, desserts) and types of diets (e.g., low-calorie, vegetarian). These recipes are helpful when certain items are on sale or in season and you would like some information on how to cook them. Specialty cookbooks can also give needed lessons in areas one is unfamiliar with or of particular interest for a special meal. Many of these books will give general preparations, methods, processes, and ingredients that can enhance the flavor of an unfamiliar food.

Now and then the sale sign says, "$3.99/lb. for salmon—½ or whole." How can you resist? At that moment you need to become a salmon expert. Get your fish cookbooks from the library, read the salmon recipes first, then the recipes for similar firm flesh fish such as halibut. You might want to prepare the recipe for which you already have the most ingredients. The other recipes, by merely presenting other ingredients to choose from, can give you the opportunity to substitute or add. When an idea clicks and a new taste has been achieved, this concept of culling from a variety of sources will lead to a repertoire of ideas that can eventually be used in lieu of a recipe.

Magazines are a wonderful way of keeping up with the latest culinary trends. Sensorial experiences are yours while glancing through the pages of photographs of gourmet foods and luscious settings in foreign lands: the best and most unusual restaurants in all their splendor, the most authentic and cozy out of-the-way finds are presented along with the recipes of some of their most exquisite dishes. We have had many a fantasy to organize an itinerary based on dining in restaurants featured in *Gourmet* or *Bon Appetit*.

SENSORY MODIFICATION

Learning to Cook Creatively Through Taste, Smell, Sight, Touch, and Sound

"Think with the whole body."

—Taisen Deshimaru

Every recipe starts from scratch. Intuited or planned, an experimental mix of ingredients is prepared to meet with the approval or disapproval of the senses. Ultimately the mind will analyze and synthesize until the best combination has been determined. It smells right. It tastes right. It looks right. It makes sense. That moment has been found. Everything has come together for the satori awakening.

This process begins to emerge when the senses have put the mind on notice that something important is occurring. The process is completed when the mind can define what brought the senses to life. While the core and elective use of ingredients establishes a set of guidelines, a creative flow can only occur as the mind and the senses turn their unique choice of ingredients into something special. And the more the senses are honed, stretched, and strengthened, the closer to the satori experience the cook will come. And since everyone's mind and senses differ, it becomes our personal responsibility to awaken them. Unfortunately over the years, as we have relied on the recipes of others, our senses have taken a backseat in the cooking process, putting us out of touch with our own creative potential.

"To know and to act are one in the same."
—Samurai Maxim

TASTE

All the senses come alive when involved in the art of cooking, and sometimes a clear distinction between each of them is impossible. Taste is the sense most commonly associated with food. It makes known to us the nuances and subtleties of flavors. Without this knowledge, we would not have the vocabulary to imaginatively choose electives that give variety to the core. Simply put, a highly tuned sense of taste tells us how to spice something up. And therefore the first step in the plan of sensory modification is to introduce the sense of taste to one of the most important categories of electives—spices and herbs.

Try an unfamiliar spice or herb directly on the tongue. Allow a moment for the taste to be absorbed into the mind by consciously associating the flavor with its name. For example, while tasting sage one might experience a strong earthy flavor. Note any free-flowing ideas as to where the spice might work well—stuffings, meatloaves, sausages, stews, soups, or other dishes that can take a strong spice or herb. To further the impact on the mind, one could look up the spice in a reference book. Sage comes from desert areas. It is also used by Native Americans in their cooking and healing ceremonies to ward off evil spirits. Associations like this make recall occur faster, and conscious recall is what the mind needs to make creative, flavorful decisions.

Next, combine the spice with a bit of sour cream, yogurt, or mayonnaise. Refrigerate it for a few hours for the flavor to disperse throughout the mixture. Then taste and make an evaluation of how the spice works in that particular combination—boring, wrong, intriguing. When the outcome is positive, the next step is to create a dish using what has been learned. This can be done by changing the spices in an existing recipe or by creating one's own recipe.

SMELL

Although the sense of taste provides us with the ultimate test of acceptability, the sense of smell, frequently our first contact with a food, is a most important tool in our decision-making process. Without smell, taste is reduced to the most potent of sensations. It is only with the enhancement of the olfactory nerves that taste can register the nuances and subtleties of flavors. At times it can even be a *more* versatile source of information than some of the other senses in determining the type and quality of ingredients. It can determine the spices in a pumpkin pie without taking a bite. It can forewarn of a potential health hazard in our selection of fish. One cannot take a bite out of each bakery bun to determine whether it might be worth purchasing, but if the mouth waters from the fresh aroma, a decision can be made.

For all of these reasons, the sense of smell needs to be treated with the same respect as the sense of taste for detailed experimentation. So take a spice or herb and instead of tasting it, smell it, giving plenty of time to register its aroma by itself, in a mix, and with other spices. Keep a list of new ingredients with a description of their aroma and potential uses. As with taste, smell is directly involved with the choice of the electives because it assists in changing the aroma of the core.

What is the aroma telling me now? Will those added ingredients enhance the aromatic combination? In keeping with Zen philosophy, it is the question, not the answer, that brings knowledge.

SIGHT

On its own or in a complementary role with taste and smell, the first important duty for the sense of sight is to give final approval or disapproval in every step of the cooking process so that corrections or adjustments can be made. Every mixture has its own visual integrity—its correct form, consistency, and color—which is determined in most cases by the specific amounts of necessary core ingredients. A stew, a cake, a batch of cookies, a soup, or a paté needs to look a certain way before and after it is cooked. When familiar with these basic visual properties, the sense of sight can register a yes or no in time to make an adjustment. For example, if after mixing all the ingredients for a batch of cookies the dough looks too wet, we know there is something wrong with the amount of core ingredients. Knowing the core ingredients, we can correct the problem by adding more flour until the sticky quality is removed. Had we waited for either the sense of taste or smell to raise a warning signal, it would have been too late to save the batch.

A watchful eye is also needed throughout the rest of the cooking process. Changes in color, texture, and shape relay messages as to how well the food is being cooked. Just because a recipe calls for a baking time of 30 minutes at 350° does not ensure the desired outcome. All ovens are different. The look of what is cooking can signal the end of the cooking time in any of the cooking processes—boiling, broiling, sautéing, steaming, browning, barbecuing, frying. Together, taste, touch, and sight can prevent over- or undercooking.

Using the sense of sight, one arranges and coordinates colors and textures for presentation. How food looks on the plate is important and will enhance the flavor of the food by creating a positive environment for the taste buds to go to work. Photographs from cookbooks and magazines can stimulate the imagination, but when in doubt, simplicity is the best policy.

TOUCH

The hands are the extension of the imagination, always moving sensations and concepts forward, allowing what we feel to become reality. When touch is engaged, an intimacy with the medium is ignited. If we can follow Zen Step Three and "have the heart and soul of a little child," sparks fly. Our logical mind disengages. What we feel through our hands directly stimulates our creativity.

While machines sometimes reduce parts of the cooking process to the push of a button, the hands remain an essential tool for measuring consistencies and registering tactile sensations—mixing, spreading, or beating; stickiness or crunchiness; hot or cold. The more we work with these various properties, the more technically proficient we will become and the greater control we will have over what we are making.

SOUND

Freshness is a sound. Fruits and vegetables that sound crisp will be more delicious than those that have lost the firmness that gives them that crack and snap. We've all thumped melons to determine ripeness and listened to popcorn, waiting expectantly for the last kernel to pop. The sound of pasta boiling over is one of the more distressing sounds a cook hears. Yet what sounds more festive than the pop and whoosh of a champagne cork? Some sounds in the kitchen are to be learned from; others just to be enjoyed!

CHAPTER FIVE

HOW TO DEVELOP A SIGNATURE COOKING STYLE

"The map is not the territory."

—ALFRED KORZBYSKI

LEARNING TO COOK WHILE TRAVELING

THE MORE WORDS WE ADD TO OUR VOCABULARY, THE BETTER ABLE WE ARE TO define our perceptions and express ourselves. So, too, adding to our culinary vocabulary of spices, condiments, and ingredients increases our ability to express ourselves in a way unique to us through the dishes we create. And since food is everywhere, what could be more fun than collecting this data while eating in a foreign country noted for a specific cuisine.

We tried Spain. We saw it. We whiffed it. We tasted it. There is something exciting about becoming familiar with a foreign country through its specific style of cooking, its history, cultural habits, and trends. Its cuisine can leave an indelible imprint that, once back home, will inevitably find its way into the kitchen. After eating in a number of restaurants and shopping in the country's open markets, many of these trends revealed themselves. Red is the most obvious color, which keeps repeating itself in its various tones. This is due to one of Spain's most popular spices, saffron. This spice comes from the dried stigmas of a purple-flowered crocus and has to be picked by hand, making it very expensive. Its aroma is very distinct, and the saffron flavor is very representative of the Spanish cuisine. Reds appear again in Spanish sauces, stews, and soups made with tomatoes, onions, and red and green peppers flavored so subtly with garlic.

Once at home with what we learned, the kitchen quickly came to life: saffron in soups, pastas, and couscous; tomato, onion, and pepper sauces on fish, meat, perhaps in a stuffing or . . . open your Spanish culinary dictionary and the ideas will start flowing in a way that is special to you and based on your experiences.

And look for dialects! As we moved from our first experiences, which categorized generic Spanish food, we began to explore and note the variations produced by its many regions (Galacia, Basque, Catalonia) and eventually its microcosmic individualist form, a specific restaurant and chef. Using paella, with its core of rice flavored with saffron and mixed with peas, fowl, and seafood, we could see that the electives began to vary from one region to another. The further away from the coast, the less we were apt to find a large variety of seafood. When a town was noted for a special sausage, it would inevitably find its way into the local paella.

With each meal we became aware of how subtle changes can exist without losing the thread of cultural commonality that ties it to its broader category. By bringing this awareness back into our kitchen, we have the opportunity to reinforce the relationship between individuality and cultural identification by just electing to make the slightest change of an ingredient in a recipe. This is why the Zen of cooking suggests that you can improve your vocabulary wherever your taste buds can take you.

Fortunately, the Zen of cooking does not solely depend on world travel because during the past few decades the world has increasingly come to reside in our various urban neighborhoods. Plan a trip to a local ethnic neighborhood market stocked with unusual tidbits. Choose a cuisine you enjoy and go to the library or buy a cookbook that illustrates this type of cooking. Glance through the book, jot down some of the major ingredients used in the majority of recipes, and go to the ethnic market in which they can be found.

While walking down the aisles, spend time exploring the ingredients on the labels. Buy what strikes your fancy: jars filled with unusual ingredients, bags of dried spices, fresh and exotic produce. Take a chance. Try something you can't pronounce. There is nothing to lose. When you return home, take a moment to taste a bit of what you have bought. Any spice or sauce can be used to create a new soup, casserole, or stew.

Thus, the process of cooking without recipes evolves—perceptions lead to expressions and lead to more perceptions. "Come hither, come hither," or perhaps, "Hey, bud, over here." A new tidbit will be bought, a taste bud will tingle. This is how to develop your signature cooking style.

RECOLLECTIONS OF A TRIP TO GERONA

"It is good to have an end to journey toward; but it is the journey that matters in the end."
— Ursula K. Le Guin

When we leave our "home" to explore "unknown lands" we also leave our everyday patterns behind and are therefore more apt to be in a state of mind that allows us to be guided to just that right place at that right time for something special.

In order to find such places and times, some, seeking the opportune moment, study the planets. Some, seeking to make it happen, call a travel agent and arrange for a tour. Still others, seeking one kind of pot at the end of one particular rainbow, may discover something entirely different.

Several years ago, in the small Catalonian town of Gerona, Spain, and following where our scents and tastes would lead us, we had been directed towards an obscure countryside north of Barcelona, supposedly noted for its unusually flavored meat and fish stews. After several meals had left us flat, we found ourselves on a long despairing walk through winding side streets that seemed to lead nowhere, even while we secretly hoped to find a master chef who would show us the way. Suddenly to our left appeared a butcher shop—Juan Carlos, Carneceria to the Stars. We could have sworn it wasn't there a minute before, but there it was—rabbits and chickens hanging temptingly in the window. Inside was a man, an older woman, a younger woman, and a child. It was close to closing time, and the last customers were leaving. This almost stopped us from going in, but there was something drawing us to the door.

We entered. Using what limited Catalan we had at our disposal, we told the owner that we sought the best of meats and fishes in the region of Catalonia. In broken English, he directed us just down the road to the town of Figueres, telling us to visit the home and museum of the late Salvador Dali and not to eat anything! Perhaps our language barriers were getting in the way. We tried our broken Spanish again, explaining that it wasn't the finest art we sought but regional stews with fishes and meats. After all, he was a butcher. If we sought the finest art, we would have asked at the art gallery across the street. He smiled at our frustration and gently spoke in very clear English: "Fishes and Meat. The Dali Museum in Figueres. Don't eat." We still thought he was a little off but there was also something compelling in his voice.

By the time we were finished with the magnificent museum, the message from our stomach was loud and clear: we were famished. But that other message, "Don't eat in Figueres," kept ringing in our ears. To end the stalemate between the messages, we made a mad dash back to Gerona and into the first restaurant that we came upon—too ravenous to be concerned with regional stews. We opened the menu and pointed to the special. And special it would turn out to be—a most unusual, intriguing, and obviously regional, sweet and tart salad. The freshly picked vegetables and local seafood with those particular spices were in perfect sync. It left its mark on our minds for some time to come, spontaneously emerging several months later in the form of what we have come to call our Gerona Taco (p. 134.)

And now we understood. Had we eaten in haste in Figueres, we would have had no appetite when we returned to Gerona. Knowing that we could not have the stews we sought, Juan Carlos was able to urge us towards having what was possible. So, should any scents or tastes or notions sidetrack you along the way, relax and enjoy because it's the journey, not the destination that's important.

LEARNING TO COOK
WHILE DINING OUT

Walking into a good restaurant is an inspiration. There is so much excitement and so much to see and taste that you don't want to miss anything. And, of course, this just so happens to be a great way to learn some new cooking ideas. With this in mind, you can choose a restaurant whose cuisine you may be interested in studying or even one with an open kitchen where you can watch the chefs use their culinary skills.

For cooking buffs, restaurants afford the chance to see dishes you may wish to prepare at home. These stand as the finished products of a cooking lesson in which the teacher says, "OK, here it is. Now tell me how it happened." The task is to use your ability to taste, touch, and smell and your willingness to do a little detective work to dissect a dish into its different components.

Once the dish has been tried, there will be some discernible ingredients, spices, and condiments with which you are already familiar. There will be others that you cannot recognize. This is when your waiter can be of some help: if he knows, he'll tell you, and if he doesn't, he may offer to ask the chef. Also, the menu might describe the dish by naming some of its spices.

Menus are also a good source of other information. They can help you become more proficient in planning and coordinating your own meals. Watch for interesting combinations of vegetables, meat, fruits, and grains. Become aware of how your sense of taste, touch, and smell gets involved in the selections you and others make.

Take, for example, the last time we ate lunch in a Chinese restaurant. Having selected a salad to start, we passed up vegetable dishes and opted for noodles that contrasted with and complemented the crispness of the salad. We then chose a citrus appetizer (lemon chicken) that contrasted with the blandness of the noodles.

KEEP AN OPEN PALATE

Just asking the question, "What appeals to my palate?" can lead to new combinations of dishes that you can prepare at home. After using these techniques for awhile, you may be surprised at the subtle change in your ability to discriminate and begin questioning previous definitions of culinary perfection. This will help you create a signature cooking style and heighten the enjoyment cooking brings.

SETTING UP A PERSONAL COOKING ENVIRONMENT

"How can you think and hit at the same time?"

—Yogi Berra

By the same token, how can you think and get into the flow of cooking creatively at the same time? Much better to make it easy on yourself and have everything you need at hand.

Claire was preparing a sauce one day in her sister's kitchen. As the sauce made its way from scratch to finish, she was poetry in motion. She turned to the left to stir. She twisted to the right to add. She bent here for a pan, stretched there for a mitt. Used a foot to pry open the refrigerator, and a hip to close a drawer.

Confidence abounded as she was ready for the final dash of dried herbs, watching for the critical moment when the garlic would not get overcooked and the spices could be brought to full flavor. She opened a cabinet that would have made Fibber McGee proud, stared at what appeared to be a state of disarray, and screamed, "Yikes! Lu, where's the thyme, where's the basil?"

Lucille, calmly looking up from her current writing, said, "Take down the three jars on the right and the two packets behind them and you'll find the basil. Move over four cans to the left and you'll find the thyme."

Instead of disaster, time stood still as we duetted our graceful way to the finishing touches on what remained an opportunity for a sublime sauce.

Paints and brushes, threads and needles, strings and picks, pots and pans. Whatever the medium, a handy supply of materials for creativity not only enables the inspirational moment to flow from mind to expression form but can become a source of inspiration as well. The scent of vanilla, the inventiveness of a zester, or the label on a canvas bag of Italian rice, can send a message to the furthest corners of the mind: "Use me!" When a well-stocked environment of herbs, spices, condiments, cooking staples, and tools is at the disposal of such a mind, the Zen of cooking—be it a planned meal or spur-of-the-moment delight—can only be enhanced.

CREATING A PERSONAL COOKING INVENTORY

Preparing the conditions of the kitchen to meet the spur-of-the-moment enables the cook to be more at one with the environment so that creative demands have a better chance of being met. Whether you are a novice or already have the makings of a well-stocked kitchen, start with the following list of items and add to it as you develop through your own experiences. Keep a notepad on hand in order to jot down those missing items which postponed that movement from inspirational thought to action. This wish list may include various foods, cookware, and utensils. Each acquisition will put you on the way to preparing the kind of kitchen environment you desire.

COOKWARE

12-inch nonstick skillet
8-inch sauté or omelet pan
½-quart saucepan
5½-quart casserole
9-quart stockpot for cooking soups and pasta
Steamer for cooking vegetables
Medium to Large broiler/baking dish
Nonstick cookie sheet

*U*TENSILS

Two wooden spoons
Spatula
Tongs for removing foods from pan, turning over fried foods
Colander
Large sieve
Cutting board
Medium-size whisk
Soup ladle
Good cutting knife kept sharpened

*S*PICES, *STAPLES*, *AND OTHER GOOD THINGS*
TO HAVE ON HAND

Worcestershire Sauce
Tabasco Sauce
Soy Sauce
Olive and Canola Oils
Curry Powder
Mustard—Dry and Bottled
Hot Pepper Flakes
Pignoli Nuts
Tuna Fish
Flour
Dry Yeast
Capers
Baking Powder
Baking Soda
Peanut Butter
Fresh Garlic
Parmesan Cheese

Paprika
Rice and Wine Vinegar
Wine for Cooking
Canned or Frozen Chicken Broth
Canned or Frozen Beef Broth
Tomato Paste
Sesame Seeds
Canned Anchovies or Paste
Dried Pasta
Salsa
Honey
Vanilla
Ketchup
Horseradish
Mayonnaise
Fresh and Dried Herbs
Fresh Ginger

Grains	*Beans*
Rice	Black
Couscous	Split Pea
Barley	Lentils
Oatmeal	White
Cornmeal	Pinto
Bread Crumbs	

There are so many wonderful pots and pans on the market today that it may be confusing to know just what to look for. All high-quality cookware conducts heat well—the most important characteristic—but from then on it's up to you to know what differentiates one type from another.

Copper pots are beautiful conductors but expensive, and owners run the risk of tennis elbow maintaining their sheen. Enamel over stainless steel is also lovely to look at, but if you have an electric cooktop, you must be a little more diligent because it heats up faster than the others. Anodized aluminum pots are also good but scratch easily; and aluminum leaching into the food may concern you as well. Pure stainless steel takes care of all of the above and has a good long shelf life. Because of cost and personal preference, buy one piece at a time or borrow your Aunt Mary's and see how you like it.

Good kitchen equipment can be expensive. Shop around and look for sales. Many department stores sell starter sets in which one can get most of the beginning pots and pans for not too hefty an investment. For those of you who are more adventurous or have tighter budgets, get yourself to garage sales, the Salvation Army, or restaurant/hotel supply houses. Many a good utensil and dish can be found in these places. Use catalogs, too, but make sure you can get a full refund if the item does not satisfy your needs. Such knowledge may help you make the decision of when to go the luxurious route on one item and save on another.

HERB GARDENS

Fresh and dried herbs, spices, and condiments are essential for today's creative cook. In fact, they have become the main creative

44

accent of this era's cuisine, replacing the sauces and gravies frequently dominating meals in the 1960s and 1970s. As the demand for freshness, quality, and variety in fine cuisine has grown, the herb garden has become the pride of creative cooks all over the world. Whatever is in season will set the tone for the meal.

In the past, only culinary professionals and avid gardeners knew what herbs looked like growing in the garden. Then in the 1980s, fresh herbs commanded their own section in the supermarket. Today it is not unusual for small pots of fresh basil, cilantro, scallions, thyme, and parsley to appear in farmers' markets in the spring and summer months. Herbs take almost no maintenance while adding attractive greenery to a windowsill or outside garden—a wonderful way to assure a creative touch to cooking.

Due to their fresh aroma and the potency of taste, the amount of a fresh herb needed in preparing a dish can be determined by our senses. And while the Zen way speaks of experimenting on your own, it occasionally whispers some time-saving suggestions on this topic. The leafy herbs are not as strong tasting or potent as the ones with the tiny, thick leaves that grow in dense clusters. Thyme, rosemary, and oregano are examples of the more potent herbs. They do well in soups, stuffings and casseroles, or when a long cooking time is needed. Cilantro and basil, examples of herbs that are leafy in nature and not as potent, require larger amounts added towards the end of cooking time because overcooking will destroy their flavor. These herbs can be used in salads as well.

There are no rules for combining herbs with other ingredients. Don't create any. One can get too bogged down with rules and lose the creative curiosity. Preserving the integrity of various foods requires varying amounts of seasoning. Determine the amounts using common sense and please make mistakes with the unfettered attitude recommended in Zen Step Five. Life is not a problem to be solved but a reality to experience. —Kierkegaard.

Approach herbs playfully. Experiment with them. Chopped, whole, or pureed, in marinades, sauces; in stuffings, sandwiches, or baked dishes; on eggs or in dip salads; on meat, fish, or chicken. Without complicated recipes and long procedures, the use of these herbs will bring great satisfaction.

DRIED HERBS

Dried herbs and spices are equally important to have on hand in a well-stocked kitchen. While there are literally over one hundred different kinds to choose from, the basic ten are: oregano, garlic, basil, bay leaves, cinnamon, thyme, rosemary, salt, curry, and black pepper. These are just the beginning. Start collecting. Properly preserved in an airtight container, placed in a cool, dry spot, they will keep for quite some time. To test if an herb is still potent, take a small amount and crush it between your fingers, which will release the oils, revealing if the herb still retains its flavor.

One method of collecting is to obtain all the spices of a particular cuisine. In the 1960s, New York City had yet to assimilate East Indian cooking into its cultural melting pot and the powdered curry found in the markets was quite bland. A visit to London with its many Indian restaurants awakened my taste buds, brought smoke to my breath, and piqued my curiosity about this new found delight, full of so many different flavors and sensations. An Indian cookbook explained that curry was not a single spice as I had believed but rather a mixture of cumin, tumeric, cloves, cinnamon, ginger, nutmeg, coriander, cardamon, and cayenne pepper. With this revelation in hand, I returned to a New York East Indian neighborhood and purchased large quantities of all the needed spices. I curried this and curried that and then curried some more—each time changing some of the combinations in order to experience as many different tastes as possible. Those spices kept for years in their sealed plastic containers.

Getting the best out of dried herbs requires the use of a more acute, refined sense of taste and smell than does the use of fresh herbs. A little amount can go a long way. The drying process condenses the flavor. When we put back the water during the cooking process, the flavor becomes enhanced. Therefore, after mixing a dressing, dip, or marinade, it is a good idea to let it stand for a while, allowing the dried herbs to soak up the moisture. I first learned this secret after messing up a sour cream and spinach dip with curry, dry basil, dried onions, and garlic, making the mistake of serving it right away. Needless to say, it tasted awful. The spices were still crispy and the flavor had not yet dispersed throughout the sour cream. It was a real embarrassment, although learning from the mistake more than compensated: dry spices need time to integrate with other ingredients and therefore the necessary time must be allowed for that process.

Experiment with different combinations. Take a look at the recipes in the back of the book and become acquainted with the way we have incorporated the various spices and condiments. A unique way of using a spice in a recipe will stimulate your desire to have it in your kitchen. If you are not familiar with a certain spice, use it sparingly for a while until a more intimate relationship develops. You too may find your favorite herbs that do the right thing at the right time.

SPECIALTY ITEMS AND CONDIMENTS

Having a few on hand from this category can give an exotic flair to the spontaneous meal and can contribute an unexpected flavor to simple foods such as eggs, tuna, any frozen meat or fish, and vegetables. These include jarred specialty condiments (e.g., chutneys, capers, and salsa) and spices, salad dressings, and dry soup packages. The foreign food section of the supermarket has a wide selection. They can also be found in health-food shops and gourmet markets. Additions can be made periodically because most of the items have a long shelf life and can be refrigerated for quite a while.

These items can also be helpful in stimulating an idea for a new dish. In one of the health-food stores I found an interesting jar of peanut sauce. Having had Thai lamb satay with peanut sauce, I felt it might be nice to do a leg of lamb using a peanut marinade with an herb stuffing. The store-bought marinade was an inspiration but needed some extra ingredients to enhance its flavor. The next time the dish is made, I may or may not wish to use the same jarred marinade. Some speciality items and condiments can be considered as our training wheels to be used when needed. Some of the other items in this category are new paint colors to be mixed with what we already have, thereby creating new tones and hues.

There are times when creative energy needs expression. For those with the bent, a meal cooked in the sanctuary of a transformed kitchen can become the private expression of this creativity, as it makes its way for consumption in the dining room. When such a moment arises, the well-stocked kitchen potentially offers the most fluid medium for expression, whereas a poorly stocked kitchen creates a path with too many distractions, too many bumps and potholes for the rite of passage to be smoothly and most fully traversed. The choice is yours.

THE RECIPES

MEAT AND POULTRY

"Every exit is an entry somewhere else."

—Tom Stoppard

A LITTLE BIT OF MEAT AND A WHOLE LOT OF IMAGINATION SUMS UP THE challenge of the meat preparation of today. No longer can one put a cut of meat in the oven and call it a meal. It is just not in vogue and for good reason: too much cholesterol, too much fat, too many ecological concerns over land use. Meat has come to play a supporting role in the cast of other ingredients and spices, often times inspired by an array of international cuisines and their eclectic assimilation into the American way of life.

This new approach to using meat isn't a limitation—it's an opportunity to explore in a whole new direction. While the American melting pot may have begun at Ellis Island, San Francisco Bay, and below the border, the imaginative blending of these ethnic styles with its juxtaposition of spices and ingredients has found its way into the American kitchen. The changing and switching of electives has already become an assumption. Chicken Thai Pasta, Taco Salad, Chinese Chicken Salad, Bacon and Egg Burrito are just a few dishes that are common to menus in restaurants serving what is considered "American" cuisine. By using the cooking processes and ingredients from international recipes, the imaginative flair of our contemporary chefs has pushed this phenomenon to its limit, as they have come up with combinations of spices and ingredients to create new types of dishes that depend less on meat and more on the imagination.

The following recipes will give examples of how we can adapt the spices, ingredients, and cooking procedures of international cuisines to our American menus.

The following Latin American recipe has an interesting selection of fresh fruit, dried fruit, and nuts combined with ground beef. This opens up a wide variety of possibilities. The fruit and nuts mixed with chilis and olives creates a sweet and spicy flavor with a rather unusual texture.

GROUND BEEF WITH PEARS, OLIVES, AND ALMONDS

serves 4 to 6

3	tablespoons canola oil
2	pounds ground beef—lean
¾	cup chopped scallions
2	cloves chopped garlic
3	medium tomatoes, peeled, seeded, and chopped
2	medium, firm pears, peeled, cored, and chopped
½	cup hot chili pepper salsa
½	cup seedless raisins
10	pimento-stuffed green olives, whole
½	teaspoon allspice
½	cup toasted slivered almonds

Heat 3 tablespoons of canola oil in a heavy skillet and add the ground beef, stirring until the lumps are broken up and the meat is fully cooked. Stir in the scallions and garlic. Cook 4 to 5 minutes. Add the tomatoes, pears, salsa, raisins, green olives, and allspice. Simmer uncovered over low heat for 20 minutes, stirring occasionally. Add the almonds before serving.

The dish may be served as a main course accompanied by rice and beans. Or it may be a filling for tamales, tacos, or green peppers.

It is now up to the creative cook to change these electives by choosing which nuts, which fruits, which spices, and even which meats to be used. Prunes or apricots, pignoli nuts or hazelnuts, hot curry powder, ground chicken, lamb, or turkey—all of these will render a different delicious result.

The following two recipes can be helpful as they suggest some new cooking processes. The first recipe illustrates the wonderful way a casserole can be made with eggs and cheese holding together a number of well-orchestrated ingredients. The choice of ingredients should be imaginative, and the spices distinctive so that they do not bake out and become overpowered by the cheese. This is an especially good process to use for leftover meats such as turkey, roast beef, or meat loaf. And a steak for one can make this a casserole for six.

EGGPLANT AND CHICKEN GRATIN

serves 6 to 8

3   *medium eggplants with stems removed and sliced lengthwise*
    salt
6   *tablespoons canola oil*
¼   *cup chopped onions*
2   *cups chopped tomatoes, skinless and seedless*
2   *tablespoons minced garlic*
⅓   *cup chopped fresh basil*
1   *pound chopped, cooked chicken breast*
½   *teaspoon black pepper*
1   *tablespoon good sweet Hungarian paprika*
2   *large eggs, lightly beaten*
¾   *cup grated Emmental, Swiss, or Jarlsburg cheese*

Preheat oven to 350°.

Salt the eggplant and place on paper to drain. Heat 2 tablespoons of the oil in a skillet. Add the onions and tomatoes. Sauté 5 minutes. Add the garlic, basil, and chicken. Transfer to a bowl. Add the pepper, paprika, and eggs and mix together. Wipe out the pan. Add the remaining 4 tablespoons of oil. Wash and dry the eggplant. Cook in the oil for 3 minutes per side, until tender.

Grease an 8 × 10-inch gratin dish and arrange a layer of eggplant on the bottom. Top this with a layer of chicken mixture. Continue making layers until the eggplant lands on top. Sprinkle with the cheese. Bake 35 minutes.

Here is a classic Spanish recipe which uses rice in the same way as the above recipe uses the eggs and cheese—as a unifier of the ingredients, and here again this can be a good way to use up any leftover meat or poultry.

PAELLA

serves 4 to 6

2 *pounds frying chicken, cut into 8 pieces*
1 *teaspoon salt*
1 *teaspoon black pepper*
1 *teaspoon lemon juice*
2 *cloves minced garlic*
6 *tablespoons canola oil*
2 *Italian turkey sausages cooked and sliced*
1 *cup chopped onions*
½ *cup chopped green pepper*
2 *cups uncooked rice*
½ *cup tomato sauce*
½ *pound raw shrimps, shelled and deveined*
3½ *cups boiling water, fish stock or chicken broth*
½ *teaspoon saffron*
1 *cup frozen peas*
½ *pound raw scallops*
3 *pimentos sliced*

Wash and dry the chicken. Make a paste of the salt, pepper, lemon juice, garlic, and 2 tablespoons of canola oil. Rub onto the chicken pieces. Heat the remaining oil in a large deep skillet and brown the chicken in it. Add the sausage, onions, and green pepper. Cook over low heat for 10 minutes, stirring frequently. Add the rice; cook 5 minutes.

Mix in the tomato sauce, shrimp, water or stock. and saffron. Cover and cook over medium heat 20 minutes. Stir. Add the peas and scallops, recover, and cook 5 minutes longer. Garnish with pimentos.

This next recipe was created to illustrate how ingredients from the Chinese cuisine can be substituted in the paella recipe using the same procedures as in the above Spanish recipe. (Italian, Indian, and Mexican spices and ingredients can work just as well.)

ORIENTAL ONE-POT CHICKEN

serves 6

1- to 2- *pound frying chicken, disjointed, skin removed, cut into 14 pieces*
    4 *tablespoons soy sauce*
    3 *tablespoons rice wine or sherry*
    3 *tablespoons grated fresh ginger*
    6 *garlic cloves smashed and chopped*
    2 *tablespoons sesame oil*
    4 *tablespoons peanut oil*
    1 *cup chopped red pepper*
    1 *cup chopped onions*
    2 *cups raw rice*
    4 *scallions chopped*
    ½ *cup chopped water chestnuts*
   3½ *cups boiling water*
   15 *Chinese snow peas cut into 1-inch pieces*

Marinate the chicken overnight in the soy sauce, wine, garlic, ginger, and sesame oil. Heat the peanut oil in a large deep skillet, add the chicken (reserve the marinade), and brown well on all sides. Add the peppers and onions. Cook over low heat for 10 minutes, stirring frequently. Add the rice and cook 5 minutes. Add the water and leftover marinade. Cover and cook until the liquid is absorbed. Turn mixture over from top to bottom. Add the scallions, snow peas, and water chestnuts and soy sauce to taste if needed. Recover and cook 5 minutes.

The following recipe from Mexico should be noted for its unusual blend of spices and can be used with any kind of meat and fowl.

TURKEY IN CHOCOLATE AND CHILI SAUCE

serves 6

7- to 8-	*pound turkey*
3	*bay leaves*
1	*tablespoon rosemary*
½	*cup hot salsa*
¾	*cup slivered almonds*
4	*cups chicken stock, fresh or canned, at room temperature*
1	*cup chopped scallions*
3	*medium tomatoes, peeled, seeded, and chopped, or 1 cup drained canned Italian plum tomatoes*
½	*cup currants*
2	*tablespoons toasted pumpkin seeds*
1	*tablespoon finely chopped garlic*
½	*teaspoon ground cinnamon*
½	*teaspoon ground cloves*
½	*teaspoon ground coriander seeds*
½	*teaspoon anise seeds*
1	*teaspoon salt*
¼	*teaspoon fresh ground black pepper*
6	*tablespoons olive oil*
2	*ounces unsweetened chocolate*
2	*tablespoons sesame seeds*

In a large stock pot place turkey, bay leaves, and rosemary. Cover with water. Bring to boil. Reduce heat to low and simmer for 1 hour. Turkey will be almost cooked. Set aside.

Chocolate Sauce (molé sauce): In a blender, place the salsa, almonds, 2 cups of the chicken stock, scallions, tomatoes, currants, pumpkin seeds, garlic, cinnamon, cloves, coriander, anise seeds, salt, and pepper. Blend at high speed until pureed.

Heat 2 tablespoons of olive oil in a heavy skillet. Pour in the puree, and simmer it, stirring constantly for 3 minutes. Add 2 cups of the chilled chicken stock and melt in the chocolate. Stir. Cover and set aside.

Remove the turkey from the stock pot and pat dry with paper towels. Cut into eight pieces. Heat 4 tablespoons of olive oil in a heavy 12-inch skillet. Brown the turkey pieces. Drain the fat. Pour the chocolate sauce over the turkey. Cook 30 minutes, turning the pieces now and then.

To serve: place on heated platter and sprinkle with 2 tablespoons of sesame seeds.

This recipe has a two-fold use. The spices in it can be extracted and used in other dishes, served over rice or pasta, or the whole concept can be used with different spices.

The following is an example of using the cooking procedures in the above recipe with Italian spices.

CHICKEN WITH ANCHOVY OLIVE SAUCE

serves 6

5- to 6-	*pound broiler chicken, cut in quarters*
3	*bay leaves*
1	*tablespoon rosemary*
3	*jalapeño peppers, canned*
8	*ounces black olives*
6	*anchovies*
3	*tablespoons capers*
1	*cup chopped onions, sautéed*
2	*teaspoons chopped garlic*
1	*teaspoon dried basil*
½	*cup pignoli nuts*
4	*tablespoons vegetable oil*
½	*cup chicken stock*

In a soup pot, place the chicken, bay leaves, and rosemary. Cover with water. Bring the water to a boil. Reduce heat to low and simmer for 20 minutes. Chicken will be almost cooked.

Anchovy olive sauce: In a blender, place the jalapeño peppers, black olives, anchovies, capers, onion, garlic, basil, and pignoli nuts. Blend on medium speed until smooth.

Heat 2 tablespoons of the oil in heavy 10-inch skillet; pour in the anchovy sauce and the chicken stock. Simmer for 5 minutes. Set aside.

Remove the chicken from the soup pot and pat dry with paper towels. Heat 2 tablespoons of the oil in a 12-inch skillet. Brown on all sides. Drain any fat. Pour in the anchovy sauce. Cook 10 minutes. Serve on a heated plate.

Recipes that call for stuffing—a bird, roast, pocket of veal, lamb, or steak—are excellent for learning which ingredients and spices are good for mixing into stuffings. Stuffing affords one the opportunity to extend a piece of meat with such electives as grains, vegetables, legumes, fruits, and nuts. As illustrated below, this is a way to add a touch of the unexpected.

STUFFED FLANK STEAK

serves 6

2   *½-pound flank steak*
½   *cup soy sauce*
2   *cloves minced garlic*
¾   *teaspoon freshly ground black pepper or mixed peppercorns*
1   *cup minced onions*
1   *apple, cored, skinned, and sliced thin*
½   *cup whole wheat bread crumbs*
1   *hot Italian turkey sausage, cooked and sliced*
3   *cups cooked rice*
2   *teaspoons ground sage*
4   *ounces light cream cheese*
½   *cup beer*

Have the butcher cut a pocket into the flank steak. Place it in a roasting pan and rub with soy sauce, garlic, and peppercorns.

In a heavy skillet, sauté the onion and apples until soft. Add the bread crumbs, sausage, rice, sage, cream cheese, and beer. Combine the ingredients and stuff the steaks. Use toothpicks to close the pocket. Roast in a 325° oven for 1 hour.

This recipe used a grain (rice) as the core for the stuffing. Therefore, most grains can be substituted. Change the fruit, spices, liquid—add a condiment or two and a star is born.

Ground lamb can be used as the core for stuffing a leg of lamb. This is another approach for a different type of flavor and style. It extends the meat dish and allows for a pasta or potato dish to be served on the side.

CHINESE FLAVOR STUFFED LEG OF LAMB

serves 8

1	*pound ground lean lamb*
4	*teaspoons minced garlic*
½	*cup scallions chopped fine*
1	*teaspoon Chinese hot garlic oil*
1	*tablespoon grated ginger*
1	*can water chestnuts, chopped*
½	*cup peas*
1	*egg yolk*
8 to 10	*pounds deboned leg of lamb*
¾	*cup soy sauce*
2	*tablespoons white wine*
1	*tablespoon Chinese sesame oil*

Cook the ground lamb in a heavy skillet, separating the meat until there are no chunks and the meat is no longer pink. Drain excess oil. Transfer to a bowl. Add 2 teaspoons of the garlic, the scallions, hot garlic oil, ginger, water chestnuts, and peas. Mix in the egg yolk.

Place the leg of lamb in a baking pan and place the stuffing on it. Sew up the lamb with trussing needle and white string. Mix ¼ cup soy sauce, 2 tablespoons white wine, 2 teaspoons of the minced garlic, and sesame oil. Brush mixture over the roast. Cook at 325° for 2½ hours. Baste every half hour.

Meat and fowl maintain an importance and integrity in all of the recipes and yet what makes each special is its use in relationship to other flavors and textures. Opening up the possibilities of various combinations and procedures with various combinations of ingredients opens an area of creativity.

FISH AND SEAFOOD

"Men argue; nature acts."

—VOLTAIRE

ONCE AGAIN WE ARE IN OUR FAVORITE SPOTS POISED TO LEARN A ZEN LESSON about conflict: Lucille—body on chair, elbows on table, pen in hand—is able to begin working on the latest chapter, after having just finished instructing a reluctant but ultimately compliant Claire on how to prepare one of Lucille's favorite meals—broiled salmon.

CLAIRE: "Yes, Lucille, you're right. There's nothing quite as wonderful as a piece of fresh broiled salmon."

LUCILLE: "Do you remember when we were growing up and our parents' friends would drop off the fresh salmon they had caught earlier that day? I don't think any fish has matched that taste since."

A DISMAYED CLAIRE: "Lucille, what family are you from? I don't recall any fresh salmon—just frozen fish sticks. I loved them and still do. But fresh fish growing up? You've got to be kidding!"

LUCILLE, *continuing on her own version down memory lane with pen on paper:"* . . . thoughts of that special taste straddles the fine line between distant and near, so far and few between are those actual experiences of achieving nirvana. Aah, was it real or just a dream?"

CLAIRE *surreptitiously brings out a poaching pan and, in an attempt to keep her sister preoccupied with the writing, adds:* "It was a dream but keep dreaming because frozen or fresh, fish is tricky. Fish is fickle. Fish is flexible. And if we convey it correctly to the reader, the preparation of fish can become a rite of passage—from the pan to the mouth!" she says as she slips the broiling pan back into the cabinet.

There are two stages in the process of presenting a meal in which fish plays a central role: stage one, search and seizure; stage two, the preparation of the fish as either a core or an elective.

—

STAGE ONE—SEARCH AND SEIZURE

In most cities there are fishmongers who take their work seriously and from whom an enormous amount of knowledge can be gained. They can tell you where the fish are from, which fish are the freshest, and which have been freshly frozen and defrosted; which are dry or oily, flaky or firm, and some alternative ways of cooking. Over time you will learn what to look for and what to look out for: brightly colored skin; no slime; no discoloration such as pink, yellow, or brown tones on the flesh; no pungent fishy smell; firm flesh that can even bounce back when touched; and, when purchasing whole fresh fish, clear, bright eyes, not sunken.

The most important rule: eat within two days of purchase.

And if you're looking for a creative breakthrough, the specialty fish market can have more to offer when picking up your fresh fillet for the evening. You can discover a plethora of oddities including specialized tools, charts on amounts of fat and calories in fish, free recipes to experiment with, and special spices (e.g., file gumbo, hot and spicy crab oil, Louisiana blackening spices). Who knows? In the freezer compartment you may even run across a Tilapia filet or a Louvar from Hawaii, and if you let your eyes rest on the ugliest countenance in the place you might end up with a rather sweet tasting Ocean Pout. Risk a recommendation from your fishmonger, go home and get ready for Stage Two.

STAGE TWO—COOKING METHODS

There is no big hoopla required to prepare fish as the core ingredient with few electives but it does require concentration: no long phone calls, no long baths, no long inner dialogues, but rather an acute awareness of time. Assume 10 minutes of cooking time per inch of thickness, but in any event, check the fish every 5 to 7 minutes to determine doneness. Using a fork to probe, the fish should be flaky but not dry. Squeeze some fresh lemon or lime and you are ready for the fish to stand on its own.

Just as Lucille was putting the final touches on her writing, Claire was putting the final touches on what she was now calling Claire's Best Poached Citrus Salmon.

> LUCILLE, *looking up from her writing at the plate she was about to receive:* "What is this? I thought I was getting broiled salmon, not poached! You were agreeing with me and telling the readers that there's nothing better than a fresh piece of salmon broiled!"
>
> CLAIRE, *triumphantly:* "Fooled ya, didn't I!"

To poach or not to poach? To broil or not to broil? To bake or not to bake? Those are the questions when using fish as the core ingredient. The answer is dependent on who is in control of the kitchen. When affordable and fresh, each of these cooking methods can accommodate the integrity of a fish standing alone as the center piece of a meal. When moving further away from freshness and closer to freshly frozen, a little help from its rather saucy and stocky friends may be required.

POACHING

Poaching is a quick, easy, and inexpensive way to prepare fish. If one doesn't want to plan ahead, one can have on hand a good poaching liquid (stock, court bouillon) or just prepare the liquid about half an hour before the poach.

COURT BOUILLON
(BASIC POACHING LIQUID)

makes 3 cups (can be doubled)

1¼   cups dry white wine
2½   cups water
1   large carrot, sliced thinly
1   large onion, chopped
2   sprigs fresh thyme or 1 teaspoon dried
1   bay leaf
2   sprigs rosemary
1   sprig tarragon
1   large celery stalk, sliced
    salt and fresh-ground white pepper

Put all the ingredients in a pot. Bring to boil. Simmer for 45 minutes. Strain. Use spoon to press down on solids. This bouillon can be frozen up to 3 months or refrigerated for 2 days.

To poach, take at least 3 cups of any poaching liquid (remember, spring water or even milk is just fine) and bring to boil in a large pot. If fish fillets are on the thin side, wrap the pieces in washed cheese cloth to keep them intact. Put fillets in the pot. Turn off the heat and start the timer—remember for each inch of thickness you need 10 minutes of cooking time. Remove fillets from pot, place on a clean dish towel or warmed serving plate.

CLAIRE'S BEST POACHED CITRUS SALMON

serves 3 to 4

1½ *pounds salmon fillets cut in individual servings*
3 *tablespoons lemon juice*
3 *tablespoons lime juice*
1 *cup dry white wine*
   salt and freshly ground white pepper
1 *tablespoon butter*
   chopped chives

Bring all liquids to a gentle simmer in a non-aluminum saucepan. Wrap salmon in two layers of cheese cloth (keeps the fish from falling apart). Add the fish to the pan and poach approximately 5 to 7 minutes. Remove fish from the stock. Keep warm. Bring poaching liquid to a boil and reduce by ½. Lower the heat. Whisk in the butter and chives. Salt and pepper to taste. Pour immediately over the fish.

BROILING

Make sure fish is approximately 2 to 3 inches from heating unit. Fish should be put in a greased pan or on a well-oiled broiling rack. Again, think about the cooking time in terms of the thickness of the fish (10 minutes per inch). Also basting the fish with a liquid or fat (butter oil) helps keep it from drying out. When one side is browned, turn it over and brown the other side. If your fish fillet is very thin (e.g., fillet of sole), there is no need to turn.

There are no rules, no absolutes to the taste buds. Just the choices you want to make. For instance, you can do what Lucille has done below, combining broiling and baking techniques.

LUCILLE'S BEST BROILED AND BAKED CITRUS SALMON

serves 3 to 4

1   tablespoon butter
3   tablespoons lemon juice
3   tablespoons lime juice
½   cup dry white wine
1   tablespoon olive oil
1   teaspoon salt
1¼   pound salmon or any oily fish fillets
      chopped chives

Melt butter. Put all ingredients except the fish in a small glass or enamel bowl. Mix well. Pour over the fillets. Marinate 10 minutes. Bake in 350° oven for 10 minutes. Then place it 2 to 3 inches from the broiler for 3 to 4 minutes until crispy. Sprinkle with chives.

If you have a bent towards sauces or want to add some zip, take butter or mayonnaise and add some spices or fresh herbs, stir and baste. Or, for example, try snapper, mild and fairly lean, which is good when broiled and then topped with a soy ginger scallion sauce.

SOY GINGER SCALLION SAUCE

1   tablespoon soy sauce
⅓   cup rice wine vinegar
1   scallion chopped
1   ½-inch piece of fresh ginger minced
2   tablespoons sesame oil

Mix the ingredients together. The sauce can be drizzled on the fish rather than entirely coating it.

FRYING

You can add a new dimension to your typical flour-and-egg-and-bread-crumb coating to fried fish by experimenting with other flours and grains. Use whole wheat flour mixed with cornmeal, or ground oat flakes mixed with oatbran. You can use milk, a beaten egg, or just egg whites to coat the fish piece. The following recipe can be used as a guide for your choice of ingredients.

BASIC CRISPY CRUST

serves 4

1½   *pounds cod cut into 1-inch squares or strips*
¼   *cup oatbran flakes*
¼   *cup cornmeal*
½   *cup unbleached flour*
1   *egg and one egg white*
1   *teaspoon salt*
1   *teaspoon pepper*
2   *teaspoons garlic powder*
2   *teaspoons onion salt*
2   *teaspoons dried rosemary*
2   *teaspoons dried oregano*
1   *cup canola or olive oil*

Mix all the dry ingredients into a bowl. Heat a large nonstick skillet with oil to almost smoking. Beat the egg and egg white in a bowl. Add the fish pieces, toss, and coat. Put half the fish into a skillet, let it brown, then remove with a slotted spoon and repeat for the remaining half of the coated fish. Serve immediately.

A quick, easy, and calorically correct way to eat fish, where crispiness replaces crustiness, is the stir fry.

STIR FRY HALIBUT WITH CHINESE BLACK BEAN SAUCE

serves 4 to 6

2   *pounds firm flesh fish (halibut, swordfish, cod)*
2   *tablespoons peanut or canola oil*
2   *tablespoons preserved salted black beans, rinsed, drained,
       and minced (available in Oriental markets)*
3   *cloves of garlic, mashed*
2   *scallions, chopped*
1   *tablespoon minced fresh ginger*
2   *tablespoons chopped fresh cilantro*
½   *cup chicken stock*
2   *tablespoons sesame oil*
1   *teaspoon black pepper*
1   *teaspoon sugar*
2   *tablespoons soy sauce*
1   *tablespoon arrowroot or cornstarch mixed
       with 3 tablespoons of water*

Cut the fish into bite-sized pieces. Heat the peanut oil in a heavy skillet or wok over high heat. Add the fish, half a batch at a time. Stir fry for 2 to 3 minutes. Remove with a slotted spoon. Repeat for second batch.

Prepare the sauce by lowering the heat under the wok or skillet and sauté the black beans, garlic, scallions, ginger, and cilantro for 1 to 2 minutes. Add the chicken stock, sesame oil, pepper, sugar, and soy sauce. Stir until sauce is well blended. Add the arrowroot and cook until sauce thickens.

Return fish to the wok or skillet and baste sauce over the fish. This sauce can also be served on pasta, rice, or couscous.

CLAIRE, *taking her turn with pen in hand writes:* "Fish can also be used as a delightfully diverse elective, supporting the other core components in the dish, adding texture, viscosity, and a complementary flavor to soups, stews, and casseroles. This can be seen in the following three recipes."

LUCILLE: "No, no, fish in a stew or a chowder is not an elective. It's part of the core!"

CLAIRE: "Oh? Then you mean those two minute pieces of clam in a can of Campbell's Clam Chowder made for part of the core?"

LUCILLE: "Just because they called it clam chowder didn't make it so. If it had been chowder it would have had the fish. It's core to me."

CHOWDERS

Fish lover or not, chowder is the way to go.

Any amount of fish can be used in a chowder; 1 type or 10 different varieties—all shrimp, all clams, a mixture of both, or try those large, tasty New Zealand mussels. It's up to your taste buds. Choose your own univalves, bivalves, crustaceans, cephalopods, fin fish, and add to the following recipes.

RED CHOWDER

serves 4 to 6

2	tablespoons olive oil, or any vegetable oil
2	large leeks—white only, well-rinsed to remove sand, pat dry
4	celery stalks with leaves, chopped
1	green bell pepper, chopped
4	cloves garlic, mashed and chopped
2	teaspoons dried thyme
2	teaspoons oregano
2	bay leaves
28-ounce	canned Italian plum tomatoes with juice
5 to 6	new red potatoes, cubed
2	teaspoons salt
4½	cups fish stock or 3 cups chicken stock plus 1 cup clam juice
1½	pounds nonoily fish (swordfish, monk fish) cut into small pieces

In a large pot, heat the oil, then add the leeks, celery, bell pepper, and garlic, thyme, oregano, bay leaves and sauté about 5 minutes. Stir in the tomatoes. Sauté 3 to 4 more minutes. Add the potatoes, salt, and stock, or clam juice. Simmer about 45 minutes (stir every 15 minutes). Check to see if potatoes are cooked. Add the fish chunks and cook 10 more minutes. Check seasonings. Remove the bay leaf. Serve immediately or cover and refrigerate if you do not use it that day.

The basic red chowder recipe is predominantly stock, vegetables, fish, and seasonings. In order to convert this into the famous New England clam chowder, just add cream, milk, butter and some thickener (flour or arrowroot and remove the tomatoes).

BASIC WHITE OR CREAM CHOWDER

serves 4–6

2   *leeks, white parts only*
2   *stalks celery, chopped*
1   *pound new red potatoes, cut into 1-inch cubes*
1   *cup milk*
1   *cup half-and-half*
4   *tablespoons butter*
1   *quart fish stock*
1   *sprig fresh thyme or 2 teaspoons dried*
1   *tablespoon arrowroot or cornstarch*
    fish, for quantity (approx. 2 pounds)
    fresh chopped parsley or chives
    salt and white pepper

In a large saucepan, sauté the leeks and celery in butter for 3 minutes. Add the potatoes, milk, half-and-half, fish stock, and thyme. Simmer 20 minutes until potatoes are done. Add a small amount of arrowroot to thicken if necessary. Remember chowders do not have to be thick and pasty. Then add fish(es) of choice. Stir and cook through, 4 to 6 more minutes. Serve sprinkled with chopped parsley or chives. Salt and pepper to taste.

For a low-fat chowder, substitute low-fat milk for the half-and-half cream and milk. Use 2 tablespoons of butter and 1 tablespoon of light olive oil instead of 4 tablespoons of butter.

These two recipes are guidelines for the many available possibilities. Add your own favorite spices, vegetables, or liquid. For example, if you don't like the basic red or white chowder, create a green chowder using puréed spinach and basil. Or why not Thai Chowder with coconut milk, Thai chili paste, and a hint of lemon grass?

GENERIC FISH CASSEROLE

serves 6

1½   *pounds of fish (according to personal preference)*
         cut into 1-inch squares
  1   *cup bread crumbs*
  2   *cups chopped vegetables (celery, carrots, zucchini)*
  1   *egg plus 1 egg white (or 2 eggs)*
  1   *cup grated cheese (cheddar, jack, Jarlsburg)*
  ½   *cup butter, oil, or salad dressing*
  1   *teaspoon salt*
  1   *teaspoon pepper*
  2   *teaspoons dried or fresh tarragon*
  ½   *cup fish stock, chicken stock or clam juice*
  2   *teaspoons fresh or dried dill*
  1   *medium onion or 2 scallions, chopped*

Preheat oven to 400°. Stir all ingredients together in a large bowl and pour into a greased 1½ quart casserole dish. Bake 20 to 25 minutes.

SALADS

"As we acquire more knowledge, things do not become more comprehensible but more mysterious."

—WILL DURANT

Can a salad be defined? We tried.

LUCILLE: "Anything with more than one ingredient."

CLAIRE: "That would make steak and potatoes a salad."

———

LUCILLE: "Actually, you can have a salad of just lettuce so it can be just one ingredient. But we've got to give them some structural parts to work with. They need to know about the food groups."

CLAIRE: "What are we going to say: they can choose from meats and fish, grains, vegetables, and flowers . . . so what does that tell them?"

LUCILLE: "If we can't define a salad we must give them some guidelines. Otherwise the subject remains too amorphous and they won't feel centered."

CLAIRE, *frustrated by her sister's contemplative nature:* "Let's just tell them one way to learn about salads is to take all of the ingredients of all the salads they've ever made, mix them up in a bowl, pull out handfuls of randomly selected items, and it'll work as a salad as long as you do it with imagination!"

LUCILLE, *sparked by her sister's jibes into a moment of inspiration:* "It's coming together. I've got it!" And from mind to pen came the following:

> "Thus, we have the creative challenge of the salad in hand. It is an indefinable quantity and mix of anything edible. It is without boundaries and therefore has no integrity of its own and yet it is recognizable. It is the cook who must give it integrity—who must create the mix that emerges from the depths of the soul, finding expression in that special sensation of tastes, textures, and sights!"

Because a salad has no definition, it requires that the cook choose with instinct and conscious knowledge what that particular salad is to do in the overall course of the meal. The salad is the flexible part of a meal that can be called upon to lead or follow any other part. Entree, side dish, after dinner, or appetizer—the salad has no inherent territory of its own and yet is always capable of feeling at home. It is free from constraints but has no comforting limits and therefore needs the cook to provide them.

By bringing an in-depth knowledge of ingredients and a sensitivity to taste, texture, and color to it, an empty bowl can be transformed into a salivating salad. Preparing a delicate, flaky poached fish as a main course? Try a rice salad with crisp red, yellow, and green peppers to add some texture and color. Or perhaps a strong fennel and sweet beet salad will complement a mild roast chicken or lamb roast. A main course salad consisting of potatoes, grilled turkey, peas, scallions, arugula, and taco chips could be topped off with light balsamic vinaigrette using Chinese sesame oil.

CLAIRE: "Hey, it just hit me that there is always something crispy, something that goes snap in a salad bowl!"

LUCILLE, *shoulders shrugging:* "No, that's not true. Just look at the warm shrimp salad on page 73."

CLAIRE, *truth perhaps taking a backseat to the desire for victory:* "That's not a salad, that's an appetizer."

LUCILLE: "An appetizer only tells when, not what . . ."

By the time we had finished, it was clear that a salad could be hot or cold, with or without a dressing, with or without greens, a main dish or an appetizer. It could be anything or everything. Look at the ingredients from the recipes on the following pages and you can begin to see how a salad can be, perhaps, the most challenging and potentially rewarding part of a meal.

CORN, BLACKBEAN, AND JICAMA SALAD WITH SPICY CHILI DRESSING

serves **4**

DRESSING

1   tablespoon chili powder
½   cup canola oil
2   teaspoons salt
2   teaspoons black pepper
2   large cloves of garlic, minced
⅓   cup red wine vinegar
1   small jalapeño pepper, chopped, seeded (optional) (use rubber gloves)

In a small bowl, blend in all the ingredients except the oil. Whisk in oil a little at a time. Set aside.

SALAD

3   ears fresh corn or 16 ounces canned corn, drained
2   15 oz. canned black beans, drained and rinsed well
1   large green pepper, diced in 1-inch squares
1   medium jicama or 2 large celery stalks cut into 1-inch pieces
2   scallions, chopped
½   cup good green olives, chopped and pitted

Steam the corn and remove kernels from the cob. In a large bowl, mix the corn, black beans, pepper, jicama, scallions, and olives. Pour the dressing over this mixture. Refrigerate at least 1 hour before serving.

WARM SHRIMP SALAD WITH TOMATOES AND FETA

2 servings (can be doubled)

10   cherry tomatoes, halved
½   cup bean sprouts
¼   cup dry white wine
½   cup chicken broth—fresh or canned
1   large shallot, minced
1   clove garlic
10   uncooked medium shrimp, peeled and deveined
3   ounces feta cheese, crumbled

In a large bowl, combine the tomatoes and bean sprouts.

Heat the wine, broth, shallots, and garlic in a medium-size pan for 10 minutes. Let the stock reduce by ⅓. Add the shrimp and cook 2 to 3 minutes on each side. Remove the shrimp. Cook the "dressing" another 5 minutes. Let the dressing cool. Stir in the crumbled feta, tomatoes, and bean sprouts. Put shrimp in bowl. Ladle dressing over shrimp salad. May be served alone or on a bed of greens.

FRIED OKRA AND PEPPER SALAD

2 servings

DRESSING

- 1 clove pressed garlic
- ⅓ cup red wine vinegar
- 2 teaspoons ground cumin
- ⅓ cup olive oil
- 2 tablespoons finely chopped fresh coriander
  salt, pepper to taste

Prepare dressing in a small bowl. Combine all ingredients except oil. Whisk oil in. Set aside.

SALAD

- 1 cup uncooked rice
- 1 egg
- 2 tablespoons milk
- 1 cup cornmeal
- ½ cup flour
- 10 large okra spears cut into ⅓-inch rounds
  dressing
- ⅓ cup toasted sesame seeds
- ½ cup canola, peanut, or corn oil
- 1 small cucumber, sliced
- 1 scallion, sliced
- 1 large red pepper, sliced

Prepare the rice according to the package directions. Let cool on the stove. In a medium bowl, beat the egg and milk. Fill a plastic bag with cornmeal and flour. Dip all of the okra into the egg wash. Then put the pieces into the plastic bag and tilt the bag back and forth until all the pieces are coated. Heat the oil in a nonstick frying pan. Brown the okra on all sides (about 2 minutes). Drain on a paper towel. Keep the okra warm in a low heated oven until all the pieces are cooked.

In a medium bowl put the rice, cucumber, scallion, and pepper. Stir. Add the dressing and stir again. Add the okra and top with the sesame seeds. Serve immediately.

SWEET POTATO WITH CHICKEN AND ONION SALAD

serves 4

2   *large sweet potatoes*
2   *tablespoons rice wine vinegar*
1   *pound skinless, boneless chicken breast*
4   *slices thick-cut bacon (or soy bacon bits)*
½   *cup low-fat mayonnaise*
¼   *cup plain yogurt*
2   *tablespoons chopped cilantro*
    salt and pepper
2   *scallions, sliced*
1   *cup sliced celery*
1   *red pepper, diced*
2   *tablespoons toasted sesame seeds*

Steam the sweet potatoes. Let cool, then peel and cut into cubes and put in a small bowl. Sprinkle with the rice wine vinegar. Set in refrigerator to chill.

Place the chicken between two pieces of wax paper and pound down to approximately ¼ inch. Slice the chicken into strips and set aside.

In a skillet, cook the bacon, then pour out all fat except for 1 teaspoon. Drain the bacon on paper towels. Crumble.

In the same skillet, brown the chicken in the bacon fat for approximately 40 seconds on each side. Remove from the pan and place on a paper towel.

In a small bowl, mix together the mayonnaise, yogurt, and cilantro for the dressing. Add fresh pepper and salt to taste. Remove the potatoes from the refrigerator and add the scallions, celery, chicken, red pepper, and bacon. Toss with the dressing and top with sesame seeds. Serve immediately or refrigerate.

When surprise leads, creativity is sure to follow. And when irony is its witness, the brain is permanently embedded with a new way of thinking. None of the above recipes has a leaf, let alone a bed of them, in it! Paradoxical glitches abound: when we think of salads, our minds most often think of leaves and yet we do not hesitate to call the above "salads" even though they have no lettuce or leaves.

LEAVES, PETALS, AND SPRIGS

As the first step in the preparation of the coming evening's meal, Claire and Lucille were strolling on their way to the farmers' market noted for its exotic assortment of leaves, petals, and sprigs.

> CLAIRE, *casually kicking up stones like she used to do as a little girl:* "I think I want to invite the Maches, Borages, and Purslanes to dinner tonight."

> LUCILLE: "I'm not wild about them, but how about the Calendulas."

> CLAIRE: "That's okay with me as long as we include Amerantha and the Icebergs."

> LUCILLE: "The Icebergs!?! They're so boring. Always crisp, correct, and white but oh, so boring. We can't leave out the Romaines and the Bibbs."

> CLAIRE: "Do we always have to be so liberal with these upstart Greens?"

And so we debated about this taste and that color until, having successfully failed to reach a "Gentleman's Agreement," we were able to come up with a mix of new and traditional greens by grafting gardens from around the world and even a few edible flower petals.

In order to choose from the many greens now available, the first task is to learn what the choices are. For example, watercress (green), endive (white), escarole (light green), and arugula (green) are strong-flavored, peppery, and tart. They can be mixed with milder greens like amaranth (reddish green), butter lettuce (light green), romaine (green), or even iceberg (light to dark green) to provide more bulk and/or control the potency of the overall salad.

Or, the radicchio leaf imparts a lovely red coloring that could be mixed with mache (all green, small leaves), green leaf lettuce (all green), or curly endive (whitish green). The combinations will come to you as you experiment. If you want to really get provocative, delve into a package of edible flowers. They, too, can be found in many supermarkets but be careful not to eat any that have been sprayed with pesticides, and because of their delicacy in taste and texture, avoid using potent dressings on them. The following is a list of some edibles to start with:

1. Rose petals—usually fragrant and sweet.

2. Borage—bright pretty blue flower with a cucumber taste.

3. Marigold—orange or yellow flower.

4. Geranium—pretty pink flower with a variety of flavors such as lemon, mint almond.

5. Lavender—purple flower with strong lavender flavor.

6. Pansy—the easiest to find in the market, hasn't much flavor but is very pretty and comes in many different colors.

7. Violet—all of the flower including stems can be eaten and has a spicy flavor.

The creative possibilities along the path are endless and subject only to the limits of your time and desire. Perhaps the following hints might make your unique journey a little smoother:

1. Use whatever is fresh at the market whenever possible. It is sometimes worth giving up what you had in mind for something that has come into season.

2. Rinse, rinse, rinse. Don't use dirt as an ingredient to create that special crunch.

3. When choosing what kind of salad you want as a part of a whole meal, think about what color, texture, and tastes will be complementary.

4. Consider seeking out one unique ingredient for each salad that you make.

5. Crisp, cold, and dry may not make for a great personality but the qualities work wonders in a salad, especially when one wants the dressing to stick to the leaves.

6. Test your limits for possibilities by checking out one of the local salad bars that advertises 75 more selections from which to choose.

PASTA

"When you understand one thing through and through, you understand everything."

—SHUNRYU SUZUKI

It used to be in days of yore that if the pasta stuck to the wall, dinner was ready. But in the year 1 A.D. (Al Dente, that is), it was officially declared that such primitive behavior had to be halted. Nevertheless, stickiness—not in the pasta but in the sauce—remains the key to making this low-fat, high-carbohydrate treasure without a recipe.

Pasta is a neutral base which is enhanced by a creative choice of sauces, meats, spices, and vegetables. The choices are so numerous that there are hundreds of recipes devoted to various kinds of noodles. But the most important aspect in creating your own recipe is learning to prepare your ingredients to adhere to your pasta. This avoids the danger of creating a soup with soggy noodles or a paste that is so thick one loses the distinction between the taste of the sauce and the texture of the pasta.

You can find fresh or dried pasta in many shapes and sizes from the tiniest of pastas (orzo) to the largest sheets used for lasagna, cannelloni, or ravioli. The choice is personal coupled with the desired texture in the context of the sauce. For instance, the texture of the delicate angel hair pasta would be lost in a sauce that is too heavy.

Fresh pasta is always a treat but don't neglect a good, dry imported pasta. Also available are less neutral pastas with their own distinctive flavors made with herbs, pureed vegetables, or even fruit juices. Look for packaged pasta that has a sheen and is translucent.

But the big surprise when you start by thinking adhesive first, not sauce, is that a world of new possibilities opens up for you. By thinking this way your mind is freer to be creative with new ingredients. The examples below will illustrate four basic adhesives that will serve as blueprints from which you will be able to create you own unique sauces: (1) basic olive oil and tomato sauce; (2) peanut butter and tahini; (3) cream, butter, and oil; and (4) purees. Once you get the idea and master the viscosity factor, all sorts of variations will come to mind.

BASIC OLIVE OIL AND TOMATO SAUCE

serves 2 (can be doubled)

3	tablespoons olive oil
3	garlic cloves, minced fine
1	medium onion, chopped
1	tablespoon dried oregano
1	tablespoon dried basil
	salt and pepper to taste
1½	pounds tomatoes, chopped, or 3 cups chopped canned tomatoes
½	cup chicken stock or canned low-sodium broth
9	ounces of pasta (flat noodles go well with this sauce)
	freshly grated Parmesan, Reggiano, or Asiago cheese
3	tablespoons fresh chopped parsley

In a heavy skillet over low flame add the olive oil. Sauté the garlic (do not let it get dark in color or it will be bitter), then add the onions and cook until wilted. Add the parsley, oregano, and basil and stir another minute, then add the salt and pepper. Add the tomatoes and chicken broth and stir over medium heat another 5 to 10 minutes, until the sauce starts to thicken. Cook the pasta in 2 quarts of boiling water, drain well. Pour the sauce over the pasta, toss and serve with the cheese sprinkled on top.

This example uses olive oil as the adherent and flavoring. Please note that you could substitute butter or use 2 tablespoons butter and 2 tablespoons olive oil for a different type of sauce. This adhesive can be expanded on greatly by adding your own electives. For example, you may want to use any of the following with your sauce: ¾ pound ground turkey, chicken, veal, or beef (brown in a separate skillet, remove the fat, and add to sauce at the end); 1 tablespoon capers; ½ cup sliced olives; 1 to 2 teaspoons red pepper flakes; or leftover vegetables chopped.

BASIC PEANUT BUTTER ADHESIVE

serves 2 (can be doubled)

2   *tablespoons tahini (optional)*
½   *cup creamy peanut butter*
½   *cup chicken broth (heated)*
3   *tablespoons soy sauce*
2   *cloves garlic, crushed*
1   *tablespoon sesame oil*
¼   *teaspoon hot pepper flakes (optional)*
9   *ounces pasta*
¼   *cup toasted sesame seeds*
1   *cup sliced scallions*

Combine the tahini and peanut butter. Whisk all but 2 tablespoons of the chicken broth into mixture. Add soy sauce, garlic, sesame oil, and hot pepper flakes. Blend well. If necessary, add more chicken broth. This mixture produces a paste-like sauce that adheres to the pasta. The texture should be thick but not so thick that it can't be poured over pasta.

Cook the pasta and drain well. We would suggest using a flat noodle such as linguini or fettucini. However, any pasta will taste delicious with this sauce. Add the sauce to the well-drained pasta, toss well, and add the sesame seeds and scallions. Toss again gently. This pasta dish can be served hot or cold. When choosing the latter, take out of the refrigerator ½ hour before serving.

Now, experiment. Choose your own spices. Add a new twist. How about substituting ⅓ cup lemon juice for chicken broth? Claire says you've gotta put some sprouts and peas in there. She won't give up on the notion that we need some crunch with the sticky!

CREAM/BUTTER/OIL ADHESIVE

serves 2 (can be doubled)

1½ *tablespoons olive oil*
 4 *tablespoons butter*
 ¼ *cup dry white wine*
 ½ *cup heavy cream*
    salt and pepper to taste
 9 *ounces pasta*
 ½ *cup chopped fresh parsley*
    grated cheese (Parmesan, Asiago or Reggiano)

Heat the olive oil and butter in a heavy skillet. Increase the heat, then add the wine, stirring the mixture until well-blended. Lower the heat and add the cream and cook gently until the sauce thickens. Add the pepper and salt to taste. Cook the pasta and drain. Pour the sauce over the pasta and toss. Top with fresh chopped parsley and grated cheese.

An important skill to learn in this adhesive is how to heat the cream into the the oil/butter/wine mixture so that the final mixture will be thickened and warmed throughout, and neither curdled nor soupy. The key is to experiment by starting on a very low flame and consistently stirring the mixture with a wooden spoon or whisk.

Remember, this cream recipe can be made with substituting any of your own electives. Slice and brown boneless chicken breasts; add fish instead of chicken; sauté curry powder into the butter/wine mixture. Be creative and try your own combinations.

This next adherent is good for people who do not want to use any fats or oils in the cooking process. You may, however, add 1 to 2 tablespoons of olive oil if you wish.

VEGETABLE PUREE ADHERENT

1   package chopped frozen spinach or 2 bunches of
       fresh spinach washed and stems removed
½   cup chopped onion
2   cloves garlic, crushed
1   teaspoon dried basil
½   cup chicken broth, water, wine, or vegetable juice
2   large carrots sliced and steamed
½   cup fresh basil, chopped
2   tablespoons lemon juice
      salt and pepper to taste
12   ounces pasta
      toasted nuts or sesame seeds
      grated Parmesan cheese

Cook the frozen spinach or steam the fresh spinach. Cool. Squeeze out as much excess water as possible. If this is not done your sauce will be runny and not stick to your pasta. Using a small skillet, sauté the onion, garlic, and dried basil in the broth, water, juice, or wine. Put the spinach, carrots, fresh basil, and lemon juice into a blender or food processor. Add the onion/broth mixture. Salt and pepper to taste. Blend well. Cook pasta and drain. Pour sauce over the pasta. Toss and top with nuts or sesame seeds and the Parmesan cheese.

This mixture will adhere to pasta because it has been blended into a thick puree. Choose your own vegetables. Get creative and think adhesive. Substitute, add, subtract. Use pumpkin instead of carrots in the vegetable pasta. Switch cashew butter for peanut butter. Instead of tossing nuts into the vegetable pasta, puree them. "Come to think of it," Lucille says, "I'll ignore my sister and not add the sprouts and peas!"

For more on pasta, go to the last chapter, "The Lasagna Postscript."

SOUPS

"Get up and do something useful."

—HAKUIN

It has been said that the invention of the soup is right up there with the wheel and the light bulb. Nurturing, healthy, and economical, soup can be a meal in itself.

Actually we don't know if there is anything that could not go into a soup and that is why concocting a soup can be one of the more creative experiences in cooking, an exciting way to try different types of ingredients and spices. Soups can be made from one vegetable or a plethora of them, not to mention wheat products, rice, pasta, and beans in a variety of shapes, sizes, and colors. If there is a "special" in your market one day, you can make it into a pot of soup that night. Don't forget that leftovers are in the soup business, too.

Late one wintry afternoon about 10 years ago, we had an unexpected request for an extra dinner guest when there were only enough lamb chops for two. We were able to grant the request because in the winter months we always have on hand a supply of turnips, parsnips, and rutabagas, cabbage, potatoes, and onions, which have long shelf lives. An imaginative use of these various ingredients with the two lamb chops made for a wonderful soup. With homemade bread and a salad, a meal that could have gone from a cozy winter dinner for two was easily transformed into a meal for three. The following is the recipe that emerged.

SPUR OF THE MOMENT LAMB CHOP SOUP WITH WINTER VEGETABLES AND BARLEY

serves 3 to 4

2   *teaspoons dry sage*
1   *teaspoon rosemary*
1   *onion, chopped*
2   *tablespoons canola oil*
2   *lamb loin chops, meat cut from bone into small pieces*
½   *white cabbage, chopped*
1   *turnip, chopped*
2   *diced potatoes*
3   *carrots, sliced*
2   *stalks celery, chopped*
1   *teaspoon winter savory*
2   *quarts bottled or filtered water*
2   *cups beer*
½   *cup cranberry juice*
    soy sauce to taste
½   *cup salsa*
¾   *cup barley*
2   *zucchinis, sliced*
1   *cup frozen peas*
10   *fresh basil leaves, chopped*

In a 4-quart stockpot, sauté the sage, rosemary, and onion in the canola oil until soft. Add all the remaining ingredients except the zucchini, peas, and fresh basil. Simmer 1 hour and 20 minutes. Correct the seasoning, add more if needed. Then add the zucchini, peas, and fresh basil. Turn off the heat. Let stand 1 hour. Reheat before serving.

Understanding what is necessary to construct a soup will enable you to make a spur of the moment change in a dinner plan or follow an inspiration. By analyzing the recipe, we can find the primary elements that are basic to any soup and, with this knowledge, practice making soups without recipes.

SOUP BUILDING

The composition of the above recipe can be divided into the following categories: (1) the main bulk of the ingredients; (2) the spices; (3) the necessary liquid. No matter how it is analyzed, assume that building a soup can take anywhere from 10 minutes to 2½ hours.

1. **The Ingredients.** Grains, beans, and pasta; meat, fish, and poultry; vegetables and fruit. They may be cooked or uncooked. This includes any leftovers. Ingredients chosen will have different cooking times, so be sure to allow the right cooking time for each item.

2. **The Spices.** Generally, soups require a lot of seasoning or they can be rather bland. Choose the spices and herbs (fresh and/or dried) carefully so that they will accent the ingredients. But don't be afraid to experiment. One may choose to sauté the spices in some oil or butter with some vegetables such as onions, peppers, or leeks, before adding the other ingredients. Condiments and bottled delicacies (see pages 43–44, 117) are included in this category.

3. **The Liquid.** The possibilities are limitless. Either water and/or stock are necessary. Stock provides a full-bodied flavor for soups with fewer ingredients. Soups made with stock need only a short cooking time. To make the stock, use the bones and leftover parts (not fat) of any meat, fish, or poultry with celery, onions, leeks, and spices and simmer in water for 2 hours, then strain. Vegetable stock is a good alternative. Bouillon cubes and canned stock come in handy and these days can be found without salt or fat. All of these stocks can be frozen. Check your refrigerator for opened bottles of sauces and juices, these can also be considered as liquid. See what will make

an interesting combination of flavors.

The addition of a small amount of alcohol will give depth to any water or stock-based soup. Beer is a favorite, but port, brandy, vodka, gin, tequila, and vermouth will all do the job.

Some dairy products, such as butter, cream, yogurt, and cheese work well in pureed soups and add richness and body to any soup base. These are usually added in the end, when the soup is cooking on a low flame.

Garnishing a soup can add a touch of zest or color. Fresh herbs, cheese, croutons, onion, extra meat, eggs, bacon, salsa, spicy herb blends, pureed fresh herbs, or chopped nuts—whatever may give an added taste dimension. Use one or many.

The following three soup recipes illustrate how to work with the above categories.

HEARTY DINNER SOUP

serves 6 to 8

3 *tablespoons canola oil*
2 *turkey drumsticks*
2 *turkey thighs, skinned*
1 *onion, chopped*
½ *pound fresh okra, tops and tips removed, cut into ½-inch slices*
2 *carrots, chopped*
8 *cups chicken stock (see recipes on page 87)*
1 *teaspoon dried thyme*
2 *large red potatoes, coarsely diced*
1 *teaspoon dried savory*
5 *fresh tomatoes skinned, seeded, and chopped*
½ *cup grated Jarlsburg cheese*

In a 4-quart soup pot, add the oil and brown the turkey on all sides. Add the onion and sauté for 5 minutes. Add okra and carrots and sauté for 5 minutes. Put in the rest of the ingredients, cook 1 hour and let stand for half an hour. Remove any fat. Reheat if necessary. Sprinkle grated cheese on top.

This recipe produces a well-thought out soup that takes into consideration nutrition, color, and taste. In taking a look at the choice of ingredients—turkey, onion, okra, tomatoes, potatoes, and carrots—they are a nice sampling from three food groups. The greens, oranges, and reds blend together for a wonderful combination. The chicken stock was chosen because of the soup's short cooking time, and because of its rich flavor, thyme and savory were the only spices needed. This will provide a good powerful flavor to accompany the strong taste of the turkey.

When a recipe has an interesting procedure, make a note of it for future use. The following two instructions in this recipe may be useful for future soup making. The sautéing of most of the ingredients in butter and oil enhances the flavor of the soup by giving the ingredients a coat of oil and thus sealing in their flavor during the boiling process. The skimming of the fat is also important for any soup which employs meat or poultry.

SAVORY BEAN SOUP

serves 6 to 8

1½	pounds short ribs
3	bay leaves
5	cups water
5	cups tomato juice
½	cup split peas, washed
½	cup barley, washed
½	cup lentils, washed
¼	cup soy sauce
2	shallots, chopped
2	large leeks, white parts only, sliced
2	carrots, chopped
2	tablespoons jarred horseradish
1½	tablespoons hot paprika

Place the short ribs and the bay leaves in the bottom of heavy soup kettle. Add the water and tomato juice and bring to a boil. Boil 10 minutes, removing any foam as it forms.

Add the split peas, barley, lentils, soy sauce, shallots, leeks, carrots, horseradish, and paprika. Simmer for 1½ hours. Let stand half an hour. Remove any fat and the bay leaves. Serve.

A stock can be built into a soup when there is a long enough cooking time and a variety of ingredients to give the soup flavor. The above recipe is an example of this process. This stock is made by boiling the short ribs as the first step. Done in 10 minutes, this will not render as rich a flavor as a pre-prepared stock, but the barley, split peas, and lentils will contribute the rest of the needed richness.

GRANDMA'S CABBAGE SOUP

serves 6 to 8

1	*pound beef bones*
1	*smoked ham hock*
28-ounce	*can peeled tomatoes plus juice*
1	*cup white wine*
2	*quarts homemade or canned chicken stock*
1	*pound cabbage, sliced*
4	*cups quartered red potatoes*
3	*carrots, sliced*
2	*turnips, peeled and sliced*
3	*celery stalks, sliced*
1	*bouquet garni: 2 fresh sprigs each—rosemary, thyme, and parsley— tied with kitchen string*
1	*teaspoon ground chili peppers*
1	*teaspoon marjoram*
4	*cloves garlic, mashed*
2	*cups white or navy beans*

Place all the ingredients in large soup pot. Simmer for 1½ hours. Discard the bouquet garni. Let stand half an hour. Skim off any fat. Serve.

The gound chili peppers, parsley, marjoram, thyme, and garlic are all extremely interesting combinations of spices that bring about a mellow but full-bodied flavor with a zip (chili peppers). A hearty soup made from a stock with a smoked flavor (ham hock) needs this kind of excellent heavy spice statement. The garlic, chili peppers, bay leaf, and thyme are spices that will not cook out of the soup during its long cooking time of two hours. The longer the cooking time, the more spice is needed. So be aware of the time needed for your soup and choose the spices accordingly.

Looking at the selection of ingredients, spices, and liquids in a variety of recipes, and experimenting with different combinations of the three major categories, puts the potential soup maven on the right path. Claire emphasizes the use of homemade soup stock, which gives the soup its body and intense flavor. Lucille puts the emphasis on ingredients and spices, letting their blending during cooking time create the flavor. Getting familiar with the different ways these can work together is all part of the Zen of cooking.

BARBECUING AND MARINADES

"In the beginner's mind there are many possibilities, but in the expert's mind there are few."

—SHUNRYU SUZUKI

Stanley Kubrick, director of *2001: A Space Odyssey*, read the wrong books about prehistoric man. In his view, weapons symbolize the evolutionary link between ape and modern man. It was an impressive photographic image: prehistoric ape/man, in a moment of aggression, cries out in triumphant pride after bashing his enemy to death, throws his club up in the air, end over end, twirling its way through space and time until turning, by 2001, into the epitome of modern aggressive, technological man—a space ship.

With the illusion of placing responsibility for humankind's continued aggressiveness on the forces of genetics and evolution, it was easy for Kubrick and others to mistake the sparks of the open fire charcoal pit for the sparks of the battlefield, to perceive the devoured leg bone of a rather large prehistoric chicken for the battle club and, consequently, the sound of "Hmm, that tasted good!" for the cry of battle.

Now imagine the ape/man throwing the chicken leg in the air, leg bone over thigh bone, letting it twirl until it turned into . . . a skewer for barbecuing on an outdoor grill.

Although a far cry from the survival needs of our cave-dwelling ancestors, there is still nothing like the aroma of food cooking over an open fire and the images it evokes—cowboys around an open fire; husbands in aprons holding spatulas while kids demand their burgers now; a fisherman savoring his sizzling catch. An expression of American culture, it is hard to find a home or apartment or even a restaurant without some modern version of the original open-fire pit—electric barbecues, hibachis, charcoal, and mesquite grills.

From the days of yesteryear, when salting and smoking were a necessity for preservation, cooks have been adding and subtracting herbs, spices, and sauces to the main barbecued ingredients in order to arrive at just the right attack to the taste buds. While you can choose to simply enhance the basic flavor with smoke from the coals, this section offers a greater opportunity for creative expression by emphasizing the added benefits of saucing and the marinating process. If you have not put much thought or effort into the marinating process, you may not know what you have been missing until you experience the added flavor, moisture, and texture to the basic meat, fish, poultry, or vegetables you are cooking.

Here are some basic tips:

1. The denser the food being marinated, the longer it takes to marinate. Thus fish takes less time than meat or some vegetables.

2. Whatever amount you think you might need, make more sauce for basting, including enough for one last coat as it is coming off the grill.

3. The paradox of barbecuing is that the smoke adds flavor while the flame takes it away. At one end of the spectrum is a simple basting

with good olive oil or butter that enhances the basic smokey flavor; at the other, a marinade intended to alter the flavor of smoke and ingredients. When making a marinade it is better to err on overdoing the use of herbs and spices because the flame will tend to decrease the potency of the barbecue sauce or marinade quickly.

For most people, their first introduction to barbecue sauce is a jarred sweet red tomato sauce that is overly tomatoed and sugared to make its impact on the taste buds. This prepared barbecue sauce makes a good starting point, and with imagination, you can transform it into a personalized masterpiece. Make note of its ingredients and then check the refrigerator for any opened jars or bottles of juices and condiments, especially salsa, mustard, and salad dressings. Certain fresh and dry spices—e.g., sprigs of rosemary, oregano, thyme, lemon grass, mint—really penetrate the flesh and can be placed between the marinating pieces. Experiment with whatever combinations and quantities suit you, and you will have turned the ordinary into something unique and different.

Red barbecue sauces have become so habitual that we have forgotten that all marinades and barbecue sauces do not need to have a tomato base. Perhaps in your next experiment, replace tomato base with oil, herbs, spices, jellies, nut butters, and/or pureed dried fruits. The following is a favorite example and can be converted into a tomato base by adding tomato paste and molasses. The recipe is broken down into four categories—herbs and spices, liquids, condiments, and vegetable/fruit group—so substitutions can be found within each category.

CORE RECIPE FOR
ALL-PURPOSE MARINADE

makes approximately 4 cups

CATEGORY 1: HERBS AND SPICES

- 1 teaspoon dry thyme
- 1 teaspoon dry basil
- 1 teaspoon dry sage
- 1 teaspoon dry rosemary
- 10 fresh basil leaves
- 5 garlic cloves

CATEGORY 2: LIQUIDS

- ¼ cup honey
- ½ cup white wine
- 2 tablespoons tequila
- 1 cup canola or other vegetable oil
- ¼ cup soy sauce

CATEGORY 3: CONDIMENTS

- ½ cup salsa
- 4 tablespoons mustard

CATEGORY 4: VEGETABLES AND FRUITS

- ¼ cup onion, chopped
- 1 ripe persimmon, skinned

Put all the ingredients into a food processor and blend to a puree consistency. Refrigerate at least 3 hours.

This recipe has similar qualities to a salad dressing, but it is more potent and thicker in texture. The viscosity must be thick enough to adhere well during basting. All fruits, vegetables, jarred sauces, nut butters, yogurt, sour cream, and condiments, such as pickled vegetables, will help give the right viscosity.

The following is a sour cream–based marinade and sauce for poultry. Continued basting will leave an aromatic crusty shell around the bird. This should be used when barbecuing the meat on the grill over a drip pan, with the coals on the side. This indirect method is necessary because the direct flames will burn the cream mixture. As you experiment with your own recipes, you will find that the direct or indirect flame factor must be considered in order to evoke the flavor you desire.

TARRAGON SOUR CREAM MARINADE
FOR POULTRY

2 *pints sour cream*
1 *package fresh tarragon*
3 *tablespoons curry powder*
½ *onion*
5 *garlic cloves*
   soy sauce to taste
½ *cup canola or vegetable oil*

Blend all the ingredients in a food processor, then refrigerate for 3 hours. This creamy style marinade can be used with all kinds of spices and condiments. For example, remove the tarragon and curry powder and substitute fresh basil or chili powder.

Different cooking potentialities come from the gadgets and tools made for outdoor cooking and the choices for barbecue paraphernalia are almost unlimited: rotisseries, potato and corn racks, mesh fish cookers, to name but a few. Metal skewers are the most versatile— being able to mix various meat, fish, poultry, vegetables, and fruits together provides for imaginative variations. Mastery of the skewer depends on similar cooking times of the ingredients and the ability to concentrate on the regularity with which the skewers need to be turned and basted.

VEGETABLES

As an accompaniment to meat and fish, grilled vegetables do very well with a marinade. There are a few ways to barbecue vegetables: skewers placed directly on the grill or wrapped in a foil and placed either on the grill or directly in the coals. Mesh holders are available for quick turning. Potatoes, winter squash, and corn (with husks and silk removed or silk removed and husks soaked in water) can be marinated with butter, spices, salt, and pepper and wrapped in foil and cooked in the coals or on the grill. Eggplant and zucchini (lightly salted beforehand to remove some of their water), carrots, fennel stalks, scallions, leeks, large mushrooms, and large onion slices go directly on the grill, basted with an oil marinade to keep them from sticking. A nonstick cooking spray like Pam also helps. Small vegetables such as mushrooms, tomatoes, and onions (small onions must be parboiled) can go on skewers. Chili peppers should go directly on the flame to char the skin and then put into a paper bag to steam. This allows for easy removal of the skin and makes wonderful additions to salads.

Here is a recipe for an unusual salad using the above procedure.

BARBECUED VEGETABLES WITH AROMATIC CREAM SAUCE

serves 4

VEGETABLES

1 medium eggplant, sliced lengthwise in ¼-inch slices, lightly salted to
   draw out bitter juices
1 large onion, sliced
2 red peppers
½ cup all-purpose marinade (see core recipe on page 93)

Rinse the salt off the eggplant after 20 minutes. Coat the onions and
eggplant with the marinade and place on a barbecue grill. Turn and recoat
with marinade often until done.

Place the peppers skin down on the flame. When the skin is burnt,
place in a paper bag for 5 minutes. Remove peppers from bag and remove
the skin. Cut into strips.

SAUCE

¼ cup sunflower seeds
2 lemons, juiced
¼ cup tamari or soy sauce
¾ cup tofu
⅓ cup canola oil
2 cloves garlic
3 green olives
1 tablespoon capers

Put sunflower seeds, lemon juice, and tamari in blender. Blend until
smooth. Add remaining ingredients and blend.

Arrange the vegetables on a platter. Drip the sauce over top.

Mushrooms are ideal for grilling. Use all kinds and decide which
ones you like best. The large flat varieties can go directly on the grill;
the smaller ones, on skewers. Here is a unique recipe for the popular
shitake mushroom:

GRILLED SHIITAKE MUSHROOMS WITH SAUCE PIQUANT

serves 4

1   *teaspoon garlic, mashed*
¼   *apple, sliced thin*
½   *cup canola oil*
½   *cup white wine*
1   *teaspoon mustard*
1   *tablespoon capers*
1   *teaspoon dried basil*
8   *large shitake mushrooms*

In a small skillet, sauté the garlic and apple in oil for 2 minutes. Add all the ingredients except the mushrooms and sauté for 3 minutes. Let cool. Transfer to a blender and puree.

Remove the stems from the mushrooms. Brush the mushrooms with the sauce. Place on a grill and cook 2 minutes per side. When done, remove to a plate. Spoon the remaining sauce over the mushrooms.

FISH

Fish has become increasingly more popular as a healthy, low-calorie, low-fat food and grilling is one of the most popular ways to prepare it. Because of their delicate flesh, fish require a clean, well-oiled or nonstick sprayed grill. Only thick flesh fish such as swordfish, salmon, shark in ¾-inch-to-1-inch thick slices, and whole small fish, including lobster, can go directly on the grill. Large fish, which can be stuffed with herbs or your favorite stuffing, should be placed in a grilling basket. Fish fillets can be placed in foil or rolled up with herbs and tied with kitchen twine. Small shellfish can go on skewers.

Fresh tuna is delicious when grilled just to medium-rare inside. Try it with a dipping sauce of soy and lemon and a dab of wasabi, the pungent pale-green Japanese horseradish that is usually served with sushi and sashimi.

The following tuna recipe uses some traditional Japanese ingredients but is definitely out of the ordinary.

BARBECUED TUNA WITH ROASTED GARLIC SAUCE

serves 4

4 *tuna steaks, ¾-inch thick*
4 *tablespoons sesame oil*
   salt and pepper
4 *whole garlic bulbs (skins on)*
1 *tablespoon cilantro, chopped*
2 *tablespoons apple juice*
¾ *cup chicken broth*
   Tabasco to taste

Rub tuna steaks with 1 tablespoon of the oil. Rub with salt and pepper and set aside. Place whole garlic on the flame, turning occasionally for about 10 minutes. Place the tuna on the flame for a maximum of 5 minutes per side.

Place the leftover 3 tablespoons of oil and the remaining ingredients in a small saucepan. Cook until the liquid is reduced by ⅓. Add salt and pepper. Spoon the sauce over the fish. Serve with roasted garlic, which should be soft enough to be squeezed out of the bulbs onto the steaks. (If not soft enough—cut a few slits in the garlic.)

Shark, a firm-fleshed fish, is a good choice for fish kebabs. We decided to use it with a mixture of fruits and vegetables.

FISH KEBAB HAWAIIAN STYLE

serves 4

2   *pounds shark cut into 1½-inch cubes*
8   *dried apricots, soaked in water for 10 minutes*
4   *slices canned unsweetened pineapple, cut into quarters*
1   *red pepper cut into 1½-inch squares*
8   *mushrooms, stems removed*
4   *metal skewers or wooden ones that have been soaked in water*

SAUCE

10 *dried apricots, soaked in hot water for 10 minutes*
½   *onion, chopped*
2   *garlic cloves, chopped*
⅛   *cup vegetable oil*
1   *teaspoon gumbo file*
¼   *cup ketchup*
¼   *cup tomato paste*
⅛   *cup molasses*
2   *tablespoons Tabasco*
1   *teaspoon hickory smoke liquid*
2   *tablespoons coffee brewed*

To make the sauce, sauté the apricots, onion, and garlic in the oil until the onion is soft. Add the gumbo file. Sauté 1 minute, turn off the flame. Add the rest of the ingredients and mix. When liquid is cool, puree.

For the skewers, divide all the ingredients into 4 equal amounts and place on skewers alternating the ingredients. Brush each skewer with the sauce. These can either marinate a few hours or go directly on the grill. Turn often and baste.

MEATS

There is nothing quite like a porterhouse steak marinated overnight and then cooked slightly charred on the outside and tender on the inside. Some hints:

1. For a tender steak, look for well-marbled meat 1½ to 3 inches thick.

2. Steaks should be brought to room temperature before cooking.

3. Beware that salt removes the juices; do not add salt to marinades.

4. For meats such as ribs, roasts, brisket, stuffed lamb, and flank steak which have long cooking times, use the indirect flame method with the drip pan and the coals on either side, placing the meat on the rack above the pan. The charred look can be achieved in the end by putting the meat over the flame for a few minutes.

Nearly all ethnic cuisines have their favorite style of barbecue fixings that go along with the meat. Exploring some of these variations will initiate the use of some interesting spices and side dishes: Chinese spare ribs, Indian tandoori cooking, Indonesian satay, Mexican grill with salsas, Armenian shish kebab, and Middle Eastern meats with tahini and hot sauces to name a few.

Wonderful flavors emerge when stuffing is added to poultry, fish, and meat dishes. With a sharp knife or the skill of a friendly butcher, slits can form pockets which can then be filled with ethnic or personally concocted spice mixtures; kitchen strings or trusses can secure large openings. If you require the skill of a butcher you may ask him or her what cuts of meat lend themselves to stuffing.

The following is a recipe incorporating some of the above suggestions.

BARBECUED STUFFED FILET OF BEEF

serves 3 to 4

2½ *pounds fillet of beef, slit with a 3-to-4-inch pouch down the length*
½ *cup barbecue sauce*
25 *raisins*
1 *cup brandy or cognac*
2 *small cans roasted poblano chili peppers*
1 *tablespoon pine nuts*
1 *tablespoon coarsely chopped walnuts*
10 *black olives, sliced*

Coat filet with barbecue sauce. Marinate for at least 3 hours or overnight. Soak the raisins 3 hours or overnight in the brandy or cognac.

Bake the pine nuts in the oven at 375° for 5 to 7 minutes.

Layer the chili peppers, nuts, raisins, and olives in the filet pocket. Truss the pocket with toothpicks and connect with string as one does when stuffing a turkey. Place the filet on the barbecue grill and baste with the barbecue sauce. Cook for 30 minutes, turning often. Remove the trusses and string. Cut into 2-inch pieces.

GROUND MEATS

Any kind of meat can be ground for burgers. These, of course, cannot be marinated but can be mixed with a good marinade: soy sauce, mustard, garlic, and dry basil are some good additions. Because chicken and turkey have less fat, it may be necessary to add a few bread crumbs, an egg yolk, or even some ground beef in order to increase the adhesiveness. Keep the size of the burgers from 6 ounces to a ½ pound for easy turning.

One last note: A good bread or roll—sourdough to multigrain, onion to poppy seed, fresh from the bakery or homemade—should be toasted with care and considered an important part of any burger.

The following recipe mixes ground lamb and beef but could have been done with ground veal and turkey or ground chicken and pork.

HALF-AND-HALF BURGERS

serves 4

¾ *pound ground lamb (lean)*
¾ *pound ground beef (lean)*
1 *tablespoon soy sauce*
1 *tablespoon Dijon mustard*
2 *teaspoons ground rosemary*
2 *cloves garlic, put through garlic press*
4 *slices bacon, turkey, or meatless bacon*
4 *toothpicks*
4 *large slices of onion, ¼-inch thick*
   all-purpose marinade from page 93

Blend the first 6 ingredients in a bowl. Make 4 burgers, wrap bacon around each burger, and fasten with toothpicks. Place the burgers on a well-oiled grill. Baste the onions on both sides with the all-purpose marinade and place on the grill. Baste the top of the burgers. Turn until done, basting as needed.

POULTRY

This category needs the most attention on the grill. The fat from the skin tends to create flareups now and then, and the parts have to be constantly turned and basted for even cooking. Have a water spray bottle available to put out larger flames. Quartering the chicken allows for the breasts to be taken off first; the dark meat usually needs to cook longer. Small and large birds can be butterflied. For large birds, the indirect flame method should be used to prevent burning because the cooking time is long.

Start with fresh poultry, preferably those not treated with hormones or preservatives. Place on a grill, skin side down, but allow the bone side more cooking time. This keeps the meat from drying out. Invariably some parts will turn out a little dry and that is why a good marinade liberally brushed on in the end will help. Herbed sauces and salsas served with meat can also add a moist touch.

There is nothing like a grilled marinaded chicken, especially with the smoked flavor of hickory chips added to the charcoal fire.

HEAVEN-BENT BARBECUE CHICKEN

serves 6 to 8

2 to 3 *pounds chicken (skinning optional), quartered*

HERBS AND SPICES

all-purpose marinade (see page 93)
spices
1 *tablespoon winter savory*
1 *tablespoon chili mix*
1 *tablespoon cumin*
5 *garlic cloves*

LIQUIDS

1 *cup canola oil*
1 *cup beer*
¼ *cup soy sauce*
¼ *cup molasses*
½ *cup tomato sauce or marinara*

CONDIMENTS

¼ *cup chutney*

VEGETABLES AND FRUITS

¼ *onion*

Puree all ingredients in food processor. Pour ½ of the marinade, to be used later for basting, in an air-tight container. Refrigerate overnight.

Wash chicken and pat dry. Place the chicken and the remaining ½ of the marinade in a bowl or pan. Cover with plastic wrap and place in the refrigerator overnight. Remove half an hour before cooking. Soak the hickory chips in water for 20 minutes, then place on coals. Place the chicken on the grill. Turn and baste with remaining sauce until done.

Teriaki chicken breasts

serves 4 to 6

¾ *cup beer*
½ *cup rice wine vinegar*
¼ *cup Chinese sesame oil*
2 *garlic cloves, pressed*
1 *teaspoon Japanese horseradish (wasabi)*
2 *tablespoons honey*
3 *scallions, chopped*
6 *large chicken breasts,*
      skin on or removed

Combine first six ingredients in a bowl. Use half a cup to marinate the chicken overnight. Reserve the other cup. Remove chicken from the marinade and reserve the liquid for basting. Place chicken on the grill, turning often to marinate. Pour the remaining cup of marinade into a skillet, cook to reduce by one-fourth. When chicken is done, serve with rice. Garnish with scallion and the rest of the marinade.

SAUCES AND SALAD DRESSINGS

"Angels can fly because they take themselves lightly."
—G.K. Chesterton

In the contemporary style of cooking, with its respect for current health trends and the elegance of the visual presentation, food should not be overcooked nor sauces be too heavy. With an emphasis on simplicity, freshness, and lightness, traditional sauces can be transformed. Chutneys, relishes, salsas, compotes, and especially the puree and reduction sauces (such as the demi-glaze) have made interesting contributions as refreshing alternatives to the more oil, creamy, floury, and cheesy textures of the old sauces.

The following is a recipe for a low-fat and flourless demi-glaze. It is made from soup stock and takes about 4 to 5 hours and can be frozen in small containers. This is most often used as a base from which different kinds of interesting sauces can come to life.

LOW-FAT FLOURLESS DEMI-GLAZE

2   shallots
1   celery, chopped
1   carrot, chopped
½   onion, chopped
1   leek, white part only, chopped
2   cloves garlic, chopped
½   cup vegetable oil
1   gallon beef, veal, or chicken stock
1   cup tomato puree
1   bunch parsley
4   sprigs fresh thyme
1   teaspoon crushed black pepper

Sauté the vegetables, garlic, parsley, thyme, and pepper in the oil in a 2-gallon stockpot until soft and caramelized. Add the stock and tomato puree and reduce by half, cooking about 2 hours uncovered. Strain the stock into a small pot. Cook and reduce by half again. (Now you have a ½ gallon.) Strain into a smaller pot, cook, and reduce by half. (Now you have 1 quart.) This can now be stored or frozen.

The demi-glaze can stand alone or be used as a sauce when a puree or various spices or condiments are added. Below are a few recipes showing the diversity of what can be achieved.

GARLIC SAUCE

6   *garlic cloves, chopped fine*
1   *tablespoon oil*
1   *cup demi-glaze*
1   *tablespoon heavy cream*
    salt to taste

Sauté the garlic in oil in a heavy saucepan for 2 to 3 minutes. Add the demi-glaze and heat through. Lower heat to a simmer. Add the cream and salt. Heat 2 to 3 minutes. Serve over red meat.

CAPER SAUCE

1   *cup demi-glaze*
1   *tablespoon capers*
1   *tablespoon chopped fresh parsley*
2   *tablespoons tomato puree*
2   *tablespoons dry white wine*

Heat all ingredients in a heavy saucepan over low heat. Serve over fish.

SAFFRON MUSTARD SAUCE

¼   *cup orange juice*
8   *saffron threads*
1   *tablespoon Dijon mustard*
1   *cup demi-glaze*
    salt to taste

Simmer the orange juice and saffron in a small heavy saucepan on low heat for 10 minutes. Add the mustard, demi-glaze, and salt. Heat and stir. Serve over vegetable and rice dishes.

Brown sauce with tarragon

1   *cup demi-glaze*
1   *tablespoon fresh chopped tarragon*
2   *tablespoons sour cream (low fat)*
     salt to taste

Heat demi-glaze and tarragon in a small saucepan for 4 minutes on low heat. Whisk in the sour cream and salt. Serve over lamb or turkey.

THE PUREE

The widespread home use of the food processor along with a desire to eat healthier has brought into vogue the puree as the sauce of the 1980s and 1990s. Because of its smooth viscous consistency, it does not require thickening agents although small amounts may be added. This process makes room for many possibilities. A puree can be a single vegetable, fruit, or variety thereof. It can be combined with herbs, spices, condiments, thickening agents, stocks, and glazes, thus making it very versatile.

The puree is a thin sauce, not as sticky as the sauces made from butter, cream, and flour. Because of this, it is now acceptable to place the sauce underneath or around the fish, meat, foul, grain, or vegetable.

There are four cooking methods: (1) A puree can be made from the aromatic vegetables of a roast, stew, or soup; (2) sautéing; (3) boiling; and (4) poaching in a liquid (when the ingredients are removed, the liquid is reduced and also used in the puree). Dried herbs and spices can be added with the ingredients; fresh herbs towards the end of the cooking time. Any condiments, liquids, etc. are put right into the food processor with the main ingredients.

Here is an example of a puree that can be a wonderful sauce for steamed vegetables, a garnish for pizza, or a sauce for lamb.

EGGPLANT PUREE

1   *medium eggplant, sliced*
1   *onion, sliced*
1   *garlic clove, chopped*
3   *tablespoons water*
1   *tablespoon fresh basil*
2   *tablespoons soy sauce*
5   *tablespoons low-fat demi-glaze*

Put all the ingredients except the demi-glaze in a nonstick skillet, cover, and simmer until the eggplant and onion are soft (approximately 15 to 20 minutes). There should be about 4 tablespoons of liquid remaining. If more, reduce on higher heat. Transfer the mixture to a food processor and add the demi-glaze. Puree. Return to heat to warm if necessary. Serve.

This puree is wonderful for any poached, roasted, or grilled chicken.

SUN-DRIED TOMATO PUREE

20   *sun-dried tomatoes*
¾   *cup hot chicken broth*
1   *tablespoon oil*
1   *garlic clove*
1   *teaspoon dried basil*
½   *onion, chopped*
2   *tablespoons half-and-half*

Soak the tomatoes in hot chicken broth for 15 minutes. Reserve the broth. Heat the oil in a heavy skillet and add all the ingredients except the chicken broth and half-and-half. Sauté until the onions are brown. Blend in a food processor with chicken broth and half-and-half. Then heat over low heat and serve.

Fruit Purees and Coulis

Another delicious ingredient for making a sauce is fruit. Not only delicious with cakes, pies, ice cream, or yogurt, today a fruit-based sauce can be used with meat, poultry, or fish. Popular fruits for sauces include pineapple, blueberry, orange, grape, kiwi, raspberry, banana, papaya, mango, passion fruit, apple, and apricot. A coulis is a puree that is put through a sieve to remove the skin and seeds. This is necessary for seedy fruit such as raspberries or blueberries. While some fresh fruit must be sautéed or baked to reduce the water content, dried fruit must be soaked in hot water prior to pureeing. Once readied, other ingredients can be added: egg whites, cream, milk, yogurt, liquors, reduced stock, condiments, and other purees.

RASPBERRY SAUCE PUREE FOR FISH OR CHICKEN

1   *cup raspberries, fresh or defrosted*
2   *tablespoons pine nuts*
4   *tablespoons demi-glaze*
1   *dash Tabasco sauce*

Puree the raspberries and pine nuts. Push through a sieve. Cook mixture in small saucepan over low heat, adding the demi-glaze and Tabasco. Cook 2 minutes. Serve. This sauce is wonderful with grilled salmon.

Salsa

Salsas are rich in flavor and make a wonderful healthy, low-calorie accompaniment. All it takes is a salsa and a sauce to turn any entree into a multidimensional sensorial experience. A salsa is a combination of finely chopped fruit and vegetables with dried and/or fresh herbs and spices. Other ingredients commonly used are beans, legumes, nuts, and dried fruit. The spices are extremely important, as salsas require a zest and a bite to be really right. This bite (so to speak) is elevated by allowing the salsa mixture to stand and marinate in its juices for a few hours before serving. To obtain more juice from cucumbers, tomatoes, papayas, and mangos, lightly salt after they are chopped. Some liquids often used are lemon, lime, small amounts of oil, all kinds of flavored vinegars, wine, soy sauce, fruit juices, hot sauces, vegetable juices, barbecue sauces, tomato sauces, salad dressings, any jarred tidbits, purees or relishes, or anything on the condiment list.

APPLE WALNUT SALSA FOR GRILLED SALMON

serves 4

2   *pippin apples, chopped fine*
½   *cup chopped walnuts*
⅛   *cup chopped parsley*
½   *cup smoke-flavored barbecue sauce*
    juice from ½ lime

Place all ingredients in a bowl and mix. Pour into a closed container and refrigerate for 2 hours.

CORN AND BLACK BEAN SALSA WITH SMOKED MESQUITE GREEN CHILIS
(TO ACCOMPANY ROAST CHICKEN BREASTS)

serves 6

4   *medium-hot chilis*
2   *ears cooked corn, kernels removed*
1   *8-ounce can black beans, drained*

Cook the chilis over mesquite wood chips, side down, until the skin turns black, or put the chilis on skewers or hold over flame on a gas stove until the skin blisters and turns black. Place in a paper bag for 5 minutes. Peel the skin and chop.

3   *cloves garlic, pressed*
1   *pound tomatoes, skin and seeds removed, chopped, juices retained*
½   *cup chopped cilantro*
1   *fresh red pepper, chopped*
¼   *cup white wine vinegar*
    juice of 1 lemon

Place all the ingredients in a bowl. Mix well. Cover tightly and refrigerate for 2 hours.

A sauce accompaniment should take into consideration how it relates to the meal. Color, texture, and flavor should be analyzed before choosing the spices and ingredients of the sauce. When the sauce accompaniment works, the senses are excited and the mind's curiosity stimulated to want to know what has contributed to its flavor.*

---

*See also the Melon Salsa given in Chapter 8 on page 136.

SALAD DRESSINGS

Although Roquefort, Thousand Island, ranch, blue cheese, Italian, buttermilk, Russian, French, honey mustard, and Caesar have been around for years and are served in many restaurants, the demand for imagination to rule over tradition in the last 10 years has made it necessary for new ingredients to infiltrate these dressings.

The main responsibility of a salad dressing is to bring out flavor and add a new taste dimension to the dish. As with sauces, the choice of spices, herbs, condiments, and purees creates new flavors because only a few basic ingredients can serve as the dressing base; oil with vinegar, lemon, lime, wine or juice, mayonnaise, yogurt, buttermilk, sour cream, heavy cream, and egg yolks or egg whites and purees are good for low-calorie dressings.

We can loosen our narrow concept of the salad dressing by changing the electives of a standard dressing. Let's take Thousand Island. Here is the original.

THOUSAND ISLAND DRESSING

makes 1 cup

½   *cup mayonnaise*
¼   *cup pickle relish*
¼   *cup ketchup*
2   *teaspoons Tabasco sauce*

Combine all the ingredients. Chill for 2 hours. Serve.

The following is the changed version:

SOUTHWEST THOUSAND ISLAND DRESSING

makes approximately 1 cup

½   cup mayonnaise
¼   cup salsa
¼   cup tomato sauce
1   tablespoon lime juice
2   garlic cloves, crushed

Mix all ingredients. Serve.

Let's see what can happen to the standard Italian oil-and-vinegar dressing listed below when Chinese ingredients are used as the electives.

CLASSIC ITALIAN DRESSING

makes approximately 1 cup

½   cup olive oil
½   cup vinegar, red wine, rice, etc.
1   tablespoon mustard
3   cloves garlic, crushed
1   teaspoon dried oregano
1   teaspoon dried basil
1   teaspoon dried onions
     salt and pepper to taste

Mix all ingredients. Chill 2 hours. Serve.

Here is the Chinese version:

CHINESE OIL-AND-VINEGAR DRESSING

makes approximately 1 cup

½   cup canola oil
¼   cup Chinese sesame oil
½   cup rice vinegar
¼   cup soy sauce
⅛   cup plum wine
3   cloves garlic, mashed
2   teaspoons grated fresh ginger
     dash cayenne pepper

Mix all ingredients. Chill 2 hours. Serve.

Experimenting with changing electives and adding condiments, spices, and purees to standard dressings will develop a familiarity with the many different ways ingredients blend to create nuances of flavor and consistency—for example, Caesar with pesto, Italian with mango chutney, buttermilk with curry, and oil and vinegar with roasted pepper puree.

Now we are ready to create dressings from scratch with the desired salad suggesting the ingredients for the dressing. A chopped vegetable salad served with a creamy pasta dish would go well with a light herbed dressing as a contrast to the heavy cream. A puree of scallions could be substituted for some of the oil.

LIGHT HERBED DRESSING

makes approximately 1 cup

3   scallions
5   fresh basil leaves

   2   *tablespoons vegetable oil*
   ½   *cup rice wine*
       juice of ½ lemon
   ⅛   *teaspoon fresh ground black pepper*

Puree the scallions and basil leaves. Mix all the ingredients together. Chill 2 hours. Serve.

A hearty main dish salad containing fish, meat, or poultry calls for a creamy dressing infused with a condiment or two. Try the following.

AMBROSIA DRESSING

makes 2 cups

   ¼   *cup canola oil*
   ¼   *cup nonsweetened apple sauce*
   ¼   *cup low-calorie mayonnaise*
   ¼   *cup low-calorie sour cream*
   ⅓   *cup balsamic vinegar*
   ¼   *cup crumbled blue cheese*
   ¼   *cup chopped walnuts*
   1   *teaspoon dried basil*

Mix all ingredients. Chill 2 hours. Serve.

The art of contemporary sauces and salad dressings can be bewitching. It is filled with infinite possibilities for refinement and exactitude. The challenge for the inventive cook is to move towards the mastery of this art without getting bogged down or overwhelmed by detail at the expense of the intuitive. When knowledge can be combined with a sense of what is called for, a sauce can provide a meal with an imaginative flair that becomes the contemporary chef's signature.

LIST OF INGREDIENTS FOR FLAVORING
SAUCES AND SALAD DRESSINGS

An out-of-breath Lucille has just come back from a major research project at the library and supermarket aisles with reams of paper hanging out of her brief case in one hand and an overflowing bag of groceries in the other. Giving the latter to her sister, she deftly sorts the papers into their proper categories.

Once finished, Lucille takes the groceries back and hands the papers to her sister and declares: "I did it! Here's the List! It must be the definitive study on Sauces and Dressings. The ideas are flowing with delectable possibilities."

As she makes a beeline for the kitchen, her stunned sister is trying to recover from the whirlwind.

CLAIRE, OVERWHELMED BY THE VOLUME AND WARY BY NATURE: "The List. Sounds like some kind of secret order."

LUCILLE: "Well, there is an order to it as well there should be. I never knew there were so many to choose from. Some are quite bizarre and intriguing."

This list shows the breadth and depth of the textures and flavors sauces have to offer. Most of these items came from one supermarket so one can imagine the unlimited possibilities at disposal. This list should pique the creative cook's curiosity to explore and experiment.

SPICES AND HERBS

Allspice	Bay Leaf	Basil
Borage	Cardamon	Cilantro
Chervil	Celery Salt	Cinnamon
Chili Powder	Cumin	Dill
Chives	Curry Powder	Ginger
Fennel	Garlic Salt	Mustard (dry)
Mint	Marjoram	Nutmeg
Rosemary	Oregano	Parsley
Tumeric	Tarragon	Thyme
		Winter Savory

MIXED SEASONINGS

Italian Spice	Poultry Spice	Blackened Seasoning
Mexican Seasoning	Cajun Creole	Lemon Pepper
Thai Seasoning	Salad Seasoning	Jambalaya Seasoning
Pumpkin Pie Spice	Chinese Five Spice	Garham Masala

EXTRACTS

Vanilla	Almond	Coconut
Lemon	Mint	Orange
Rum	Strawberry	

SAUCES FOR ADDED FLAVOR

Ketchup	Chutneys	Horseradish
Marinades	Garlic Sauce	Prepared Curry
Teriyaki Sauce	Tabasco	Red Chili Sauce
Sweet-and-Sour Sauce	Pineapple Salsa	Hot Pepper Salsas
Taco Sauce	Enchilada Sauce	Cocktail Sauce
Marmite	Molé	Hot-and-Spicy Sauce
Smokey Pecan Barbecue Sauce	Honey Dijon Sauce	Chicken Wing Sauce
Spaghetti Sauce		

CONDIMENTS AND JARRED INGREDIENTS

Coconut Milk
Jelly—Mint, Grape,
   Raspberry, etc.
Miso

Anchovy and Garlic Paste
Marmalade—Orange,
   Pineapple, etc.
Ground Sesame Seeds

Thai Fish Sauce
Honey
Nut Butters—
   Peanut, Cashew, etc.

MUSTARDS

Honey Dill
Dijon
Dill

Hawaiian Pineapple
Shallot

Extra Hot
Horseradish

PICKLED ITEMS

Gherkins
Marinated Eggplant
Canned Chilis

Cucumbers
Olives
Relish

Marinated Pepper
Capers

VINEGARS

Rice
White

Wine
Flavored

Red
Balsamic

LIQUIDS

Wine
Soy Sauce

Fruit Juice
Braggs Amino Acids

Beer

SYRUPS

Fruit
Marshmallow

Fudge

Caramel

Salad Dressings

Mayonnaise   Bottled Dressings

Oils

Flavored with Herbs	Peanut	Canola
Olive	Almond	Sesame
Safflower		

Thickening Agents

Sour Cream	Creme Fraiche	Cream Cheese
Yogurt	Heavy Cream	Half-and-Half Cream
Butter	Butter mixed with Flour	Egg Yolks
Cheese	Arrowroot Flour	Corn Starch
Nut Butters		

VEGETABLES

"Whatever interests, is interesting."

—William Hazlitt

Vegetables have had to struggle long and hard to make their way back into the culinary spotlight. No longer an undistinguished and unwanted interloper at the table, they have returned as a major factor in the creative cooking process.

However, overcoming their bad rap has not been easy. By the Gerber Baby Food boom of the 1940s, the curtain was closing on the time when the local market would be selling vegetables picked that day. As mass production and distribution increased, memories faded of sweet peas in the pod, tomatoes that tingled the palate, corn so sweet it could be eaten off the cob with no cooking needed.

Who could blame those reluctant kids of the 1950s and 1960s who were forced to eat their vegetables before getting dessert or leaving the table? No wonder they developed the metaphors of "vegetables" for the comatose or "turnip" for the dull-witted. Canned, overcooked, and mushy; defrosted and doused into oblivion with salt and butter sauces; or freshly picked but wilting in plastic-wrap suffocation—by the time the vegetable made it to the table in this era of darkness, flavor, texture and quite often the nutritional values for which they had been so highly touted had been lost.

But then the very same mass-production and delivery systems that almost snuffed them out brought diversely delectable vegetables from all over the world back to the American dining table. Today, thanks to ethnic markets, local farmers' markets, and specialty gardens, providing us with everything from "Maui" onions to "Chinese" broccoli, the comeback is complete.

THE PROPER ORDER OF THINGS—MASTERING THE FOUR FACTORS

Within bounds that respect a vegetable's integrity, there are four major factors that must be considered in its selection and preparation for the overall meal. Each factor will rely on the others.

FACTOR ONE.

In determining the *cooking process,* choose one that will complement the other items in the meal:
1. steam
2. stirfry
3. broil
4. fry
5. braise
6. casserole
7. boil
8. sauté
9. bake
10. charcoal
11. puree
12. sauced
13. stuffed

FACTOR TWO.

Choose a *color* that complements the overall look you want to achieve for the meal. What color would you choose to juxtapose with salmon pink?

FACTOR THREE.

Texture can range from a smooth puree to raw and crisp. If the texture of the main dish is soft you might want a crunchy vegetable complement.

FACTOR FOUR.

Degree of flavoring as determined by the use of spices, sauces, and other ingredients (e.g., bread crumbs, cheese, and nuts).

Each of the following recipes will be followed by an analysis of these four steps.

CAULIFLOWER WITH MUSTARD SAUCE AND VEGETARIAN MEAT LOAF

serves 4

VEGETARIAN MEAT LOAF

1   *medium onion, chopped*
3   *cups cooked short-grain brown rice*
1   *cup cooked lentils*
½   *cup cooked barley*
½   *cup crushed almonds*
¼   *cup soy sauce*
½   *cup low-calorie sour cream*
½   *cup plain non-fat yogurt*
½   *cup shredded carrots*
1   *egg*
2   *teaspoons ground sage*
2   *teaspoons dried oregano*
2   *tablespoons vegetable oil*
      ground black pepper to taste

Preheat the oven to 350°.

In a large skillet, sauté the onion in 1 tablespoon oil until golden brown. Turn off the heat and add the remaining ingredients, blending well. Grease a meat loaf pan and spoon in the mixture, pat down and compress. Bake 45 minutes in the oven. Cool for 20 minutes before serving.

CAULIFLOWER WITH MUSTARD SAUCE

1   *head of cauliflower*
2   *tablespoons mayonnaise (can use low-fat)*
2   *tablespoons Dijon mustard*
½   *cup toasted bread crumbs*
      salt and pepper to taste

Break the cauliflower into small florets. Steam until desired doneness. Mix the mayonnaise, mustard, salt, and pepper in a small bowl. Transfer the cauliflower to a serving dish. Spoon in the sauce and toss well. Top with the bread crumbs.

ANALYSIS

Factor one, *Cooking Process:* Steaming was chosen to keep the vegetable selection crisp in contrast with the texture of the vegetable loaf and to avoid using extra oil.

Factor two, *Color:* White cauliflower and pale yellow sauce were juxtaposed with the orange-flaked vegetable loaf.

Factor three, *Texture:* The vegetable, vegetable loaf, and mustard sauce were chosen to bring crispiness, solidity, and creaminess as the desired textural components.

Factor four, *Degree of Flavoring:* The loaf contributes subtle background for the sharp mustard accent of the sauce. Had the main dish been highly flavorable, a much milder sauce would have been chosen for the cauliflower.

POTATO PANCAKES WITH APPLE CREAM SAUCE AND STUFFED ZUCCHINI

serves 4

POTATO PANCAKES

5   medium red potatoes
½   white onion, grated
¼   cup unbleached all-purpose flour
2   eggs, beaten
½   teaspoon salt
⅓   cup canola or peanut oil

Shred the potatoes or put through a ricer and squeeze out the excess water. In a large bowl, combine all the ingredients. If mixture is too watery, add a little more flour.

Heat a large nonstick frying pan and add half of the oil. Ladle out enough of the mixture to form as many 3-inch diameter pancakes as will fit in the pan. Fry one side until golden brown, flip and cook the other side. Repeat the process until all the mixture is gone. Drain the pancakes on paper towels. Keep warm on a cookie sheet in the oven until ready to serve.

APPLE CREAM SAUCE

⅔   cup low-fat sour cream
     juice from ½ lemon
¼   of a large Granny Smith apple, skin removed
     salt and pepper to taste

Put all the ingredients in a blender. Puree until smooth. Serve sauce with the pancake and zucchini.

STUFFED ZUCCHINI

4	*medium zucchini*
5	*medium-size mushrooms*
2	*tablespoons vegetable oil*
4	*roma tomatoes or an 8-ounce can whole tomatoes, chopped*
½	*cup unseasoned bread crumbs*
2	*cloves garlic, minced*
1	*egg and 1 egg white beaten together*
1	*teaspoon Tabasco sauce*
1 to 2	*tablespoons fresh chopped herbs—oregano, tarragon, parsley, etc.*
¾	*cup grated cheese (any kind) or low-fat ricotta cheese*
	salt and pepper to taste

Preheat the oven to 350°.

Partially cook the zucchini in boiling salted water for 2 to 3 minutes. Let cool. Zucchini should still be very firm. Cut the zucchini in half and scoop out the pulp. Chop the pulp. Chop the mushrooms. In a large skillet, add the oil and sauté the pulp and mushrooms 2 to 3 minutes. Add all the other ingredients except the cheese and herbs and stir well. Let cook 3 to 4 minutes, then stir in the cheese and chopped herbs. Stuff the zucchini with the mixture and place in the oven on a greased baking dish. Bake for 25 minutes.

ANALYSIS

Factor one, *Cooking Process:* Frying was chosen to provide a crisp and heavy texture of the pancake to contrast with the lightly baked zucchini.

Factor two, *Color:* An overall presentation that could open a paint store with such colors as Zucchini Green, Pancake Brown, and Sour Cream White.

Factor three, *Texture:* The crisp, dense texture of the pancakes was chosen in contrast with the firm outer layer and the soft inner contents of the zucchini.

Factor four, *Degree of Flavoring:* A little bit of hot flavor in the zucchini versus the unspiced neutral flavor of the potato pancake unified by the tangy flavor of the sour cream sauce.

SPICY GARLIC SPINACH WITH BAKED CHICKEN BREASTS AND BROWN BASMATI RICE

serves 4

SPICY GARLIC SPINACH

2   bunches fresh spinach, stems removed, rinsed, and patted dry
1   tablespoon butter
4   cloves garlic, mashed
1   tablespoon olive oil
1   small can chopped hot jalapeño peppers or 1 small jalapeño pepper,
      seeded and chopped (If using fresh jalapeño peppers, dice ½ table-
      spoon. If using canned jalapeño peppers, use 4-ounce can. Use only
      ½ can if you want less spicy; do not use seeds)
1   teaspoon salt

Melt the butter in a small cooking pot. Add the garlic, oil, hot peppers, and salt and stir over a low flame for 2 to 3 minutes. Layer the spinach and sauce in a steamer. Steam until spinach is completely wilted. Place the spinach on a serving dish.

BAKED CHICKEN BREASTS

1   cup brown basmati rice
12 sun-dried tomatoes
½   cup lemon juice
4   medium chicken breasts
    soy sauce for basting

Preheat the oven to 375°.

Soak the sun-dried tomatoes in the lemon juice for 30 minutes. Drain the tomatoes retaining the juice. Follow the package directions for cooking

---

*Use gloves when chopping jalapeño peppers and wash all utensils and surfaces afterwards.

---

the brown rice (allow for 30 minutes). Place chicken breasts in a baking dish. Put 3 sun-dried tomatoes under the skin of each breast. Pour the remaining lemon juice over the chicken. Baste once or twice with soy sauce. Place in the oven and bake for 20 to 25 minutes until done. Put under the broiler for the last few minutes to brown the skin.

ANALYSIS

Factor one, *Cooking Process:* Steaming the spinach keeps its leafy texture and cuts down on the fat used for the overall meal. Baking was chosen to help seal the sun-dried tomato flavor into the chicken.

Factor two, *Color:* The white of the chicken breast and the unexpected red of the tomatoes under the skin contrast with the green of the spinach.

Factor three, *Texture:* The leafy texture of the spinach combines with the firmness of the breasts and the soft yet crunchy rice.

Factor four, *Degree of Flavoring:* Hot and spicy spinach, the subtle pungent flavor of the chicken, and the nutty flavor of the brown rice brings substance and life to the meal.

WALNUT SQUASH CASSEROLE, MINTED PEAS, AND LEEKS WITH LEG OF LAMB

serves 4

WALNUT SQUASH CASSEROLE

3	*pounds butter squash or any firm-flesh squash*
1	*cup unsweetened apple sauce*
1	*egg and 1 egg white, beaten together*
2	*teaspoons orange rind (use a zester)*
½	*teaspoon grated fresh nutmeg*
½	*cup chopped walnuts*

Preheat the oven to 350°.

Cut the squash into 1-inch slices. Steam the slices until soft but still holding their shape. Remove the skin and seeds. Place the squash in a blender or food processor (if neither of these are available use a potato masher). Add the remaining ingredients except the walnuts. Blend well. Pour the mixture into a greased 8 × 11-inch baking dish. Top with the walnuts and bake for 35 to 40 minutes.

MINTED PEAS AND LEEKS

serves 4

2	*10-ounce packages frozen peas*
1	*large leek or 2 small leeks*
2	*tablespoons vegetable oil*
1	*teaspoon powdered cumin*
⅔	*cup plain yogurt*
4 to 5	*fresh mint leaves*
1	*teaspoon salt*
	pinch white pepper

Put the frozen peas in a colander and run hot water over them to defrost. Shake off the excess water. Cut off the green tops from the leeks. Clean the white parts thoroughly to remove sand. Slice the leeks into ¼-inch pieces.

In a large skillet, heat the oil and add the cumin and leeks. Sauté until leeks just wilt. Add the peas and cook 2 to 3 minutes. Turn off the heat. Add the yogurt, mint, salt, and pepper. Stir well and serve immediately.

LEG OF LAMB

serves 4 to 6

4 to 6	pounds leg of lamb
	salt and freshly ground pepper to taste
12	ounces bottled dark ale

Preheat the oven to 350°.

Place the leg of lamb in a roasting pan. Salt and pepper to taste. Pour the dark ale over the leg of lamb. Roast in the oven, basting the lamb with the pan juices every 15 to 20 minutes until done. Lamb should be done in 1½ to 2 hours, when the thermometer registers 160°.

ANALYSIS

Produce the meal and let us know. Would they have been your choice of colors, textures, and flavors? Would you have used different cooking processes to achieve the same complements? How would you analyze the following three meals?

ASPARAGUS PIE WITH CRISP GREEN SALAD

serves 4 to 6

SAUCE

1	tablespoon butter
1	cup milk (non-fat or low-fat can be used)
1	tablespoon apple juice
4	tablespoons flour
1	teaspoon onion salt
	salt and pepper to taste
2 to 3	teaspoons hot paprika

Combine all the ingredients in a bowl, using a whisk to blend well. If the mixture is too thick, add more milk. Check seasonings.

ASPARAGUS PIE

2½	cups chopped asparagus (frozen may be used, defrost and drain well)
3	hard-boiled eggs
1	9-inch pie crust, baked (see Chapter 2, page 13 for recipe)
½	cup shredded cheese (mozzarella, Swiss, Jarlsburg)

Preheat the oven to 325°.

In a large pot, bring enough water to a boil for blanching the asparagus. Trim the bottom of the asparagus, removing the tough stems. Put into boiling water and cook 2 to 3 minutes. Cut the asparagus into small pieces. Slice the eggs and layer them on the bottom of the pie shell. Then add a layer of asparagus. Pour the sauce over the pie, making sure some of it reaches the bottom. Sprinkle the cheese on top. Bake for 40 minutes. Cool 10 to 15 minutes before serving.

Since you can substitute almost any vegetable or combination of herbs in this pie, what vegetables would you choose in order to achieve a different texture and degree of flavoring? Zucchini, broccoli, sliced carrots? Substitute curry for hot paprika? Add slices of onion or tomato or green peppers between layers if you like. The choices are bound only by the texture, flavoring, colors, and cooking processes. Make some changes and see what happens. You can even eliminate the crust if you are in a hurry.

CAPONATA

serves 4

2½   *pounds firm eggplants*
½   *cup peanut or canola oil (try not to use olive oil because too much of it
        is absorbed by the eggplant, and it will make your dish too oily)*
½   *cup salt*
3 to 4   *celery stalks with the leaves on*
1   *medium onion, sliced*
3   *ounces canned tomato paste*
2 to 3   *tablespoons sugar*
1   *cup red wine vinegar*
¼   *cup capers*
1   *cup green olives, pitted*
    freshly ground pepper to taste

Cut the top and bottom off of the eggplant. Dice the eggplant into cubes without peeling and put in a colander. Sprinkle salt all over the cubes to get rid of the bitter juices. Let stand 1 hour. Then rinse well and blot dry.

In a large frying pan, heat a ¼ cup of the oil and brown the cubes on all sides. Remove and drain the cubes on paper towels. In the same pan, add the celery and sauté until light brown. Remove and drain on paper towels.

In another frying pan, heat the other ¼ cup oil and sauté the onion until golden brown. Add the tomato paste and dilute with a little water. Add the sugar, vinegar, capers, olives, eggplant, and celery. Check the seasonings. Add salt and pepper to taste. Simmer 10 to 15 minutes. Let cool. Serve immediately or refrigerate in a well-sealed container.

How would you make best use of this dish in order to complement its sautéed textures, colors, and flavoring? Would you use it as a main course or hors d'oeuvre? Would you serve it with bread or a grain? Lucille loves this heaped high on French bread; Claire serves it cold with fluffy couscous. There is no one right answer. That's the beauty of the Zen of cooking.

CHAPTER EIGHT

THE BEST OF TWO ZEN COOKS

Lucille and Claire's Most Delicious, Most Inventive Culinary Creations

"Go—not knowing where. Bring—not knowing what. The path is long, the way unknown."

—Russian Fairy Tale

WE HAVE BEEN COOKING WITH THE ZEN APPROACH OUTLINED IN THIS BOOK FOR many years, and many delicious and soul satisfying creations have resulted. Here are some of our favorites to inspire you to create some of your own.

The inspiration for the following taco recipe came from a restaurant in the Catalonian town of Girona, Spain. We sampled a delectable diced melon and shrimp salad in an oil and vinegar dressing. It looked like a salsa of sorts but it didn't have any heat. However, it had a bite to it created by the contrast of the sweetness of the melon and the tartness of the vinegar. The combined texture of the melon and the shrimp was also intriguing.

When we returned home to our kitchen, we concocted a shrimp taco that incorporated the Girona experience. By replacing the vinegar with cayenne pepper, adding garlic to the sautéed shrimp, and placing it all on a bed of black beans wrapped in a corn tortilla, we had maintained its Spanish integrity but added a Latin American influence.

GIRONA TACOS WITH MELON SALSA

serves 4

1   *tablespoon butter*
4   *garlic cloves, mashed*
8   *medium shrimp—cleaned, shelled*
¾   *cup black beans*
1   *can chicken broth*
1½ *cups water*
2   *tablespoons oregano*
2   *tablespoons cumin*
3   *teaspoons salt*
2   *tablespoons olive oil*
½   *sweet onion*
½   *cantaloupe*
¼   *teaspoon cayenne pepper*
8   *soft tortillas (corn or flour)*
1   *cup finely shredded iceberg lettuce*
½   *cup chopped cilantro*

Melt the butter in a small skillet. On low heat, add 2 mashed garlic cloves and shrimp and sauté approximately 2 minutes on each side. Transfer the mixture to a small bowl. Refrigerate 2 hours while the beans are cooking.

BEANS

Cover the beans with water and soak refrigerated overnight. Remove the beans from refrigerator and place in a large enamel pot. Pour the can of chicken broth and 1½ cups water over the beans. Add the oregano, cumin, the remaining garlic cloves, and 2 teaspoons salt. Bring the beans to a boil and simmer 1½ to 2 hours until the beans are tender. With a potato masher, or the back of a fork, mash half of the beans to create a puree. Blend back into the rest of the beans, adding 1 tablespoon of olive oil. Mixture should resemble a thick stew.

SALSA

Dice the onion and melon. Combine ⅛ teaspoon cayenne pepper with 1 teaspoon salt and sprinkle over the onions and melons and mix together.

TO ASSEMBLE TACOS

Remove the shrimp from the refrigerator and cut each into 3 to 4 chunks, put shrimp in small skillet, reheat gently 2 to 3 minutes. Lay the tacos out flat, place 2 full tablespoons of black beans in the center, then layer consecutively the shredded lettuce, shrimp mixture, melon salsa, and top with chopped fresh cilantro. Roll up and eat.

POACHED SALMON WITH SPINACH-BASIL DRESSING

serves 4 to 5

The spinach-basil puree Lucille became addicted to was introduced to her at some dinner somewhere in Los Angeles. For a period of weeks thereafter, she became consumed with the desire that all fish and vegetables *chez moi* would find their companion in this delicious treat.

As the original excitement began to wane after countless preparations, the need for something new emerged. Save the flavor, change the texture. It came to me while preparing the puree for a whole salmon. By just adding bread crumbs and egg yolks, I could turn the puree into a mousse-like stuffing.

1   *4- to 5-pound salmon, center bone removed (head on or off is optional)*
1   *bunch scallions, chopped*
4   *cloves chopped garlic*
2   *10-ounce packages chopped frozen spinach, defrosted, drained, liquid reserved*
3   *cups fresh basil*
2   *tablespoons soy sauce*
2   *cups fresh bread crumbs*
2   *egg yolks*

1   *bunch parsley*
3   *tablespoons olive oil*

FISH MARINADE

3   *tablespoons olive oil*
3   *tablespoons vinegar*
1   *teaspoon Dijon mustard*
1   *sprig rosemary*

Blend all the marinade ingredients together in a food processor.

PREPARE FISH FOR DRESSING

On a large baking sheet or pan, place one layer of aluminum foil and one layer of clear plastic wrap, enough to cover salmon. Wash salmon, pat dry, and place in center of clear plastic wrap. Brush generously with marinade.

DRESSING

In a large skillet, heat 3 tablespoons olive oil and the scallions, garlic, spinach, and basil. Stir to combine and simmer covered for 5 minutes. Add the soy sauce. Put the mixture into the food processor and puree. Add the bread crumbs and egg yolks until mixture is firm. If it's too watery, add more bread crumbs; if it's too dry, add some spinach juice.

Spoon the dressing into the cavity of the fish. Press the foil tightly to cover the fish and seal the seams. Refrigerate overnight or for 6 to 8 hours.

When ready to cook, remove the fish from the refrigerator. Preheat the oven to 350°. Place on the middle rack and bake 1 hour or until done.

Transfer to a large plate and garnish with the parsley.

Lucille remembers: I was reminded of an aromatically spiced dish I used to make when I tasted sautéed baby octopus in a Los Angeles restaurant. What a delight to find the addition of capers, lime juice, and extremely plump white raisins in this sauce.

Practicing what we have been preaching, I cajoled the waiter into revealing that the plumpness was an outcome of a good long soak in heated fruit juice.

What follows is the evolution of the octopus dish into a new variation with skewered seafood and, of course, plump raisins . . . isn't imitation the highest form of flattery?

SEAFOOD EN BROCHETTE WITH TEN-SPICE SAUCE

½   *cup white raisins*
½   *cup fruit juice*
1   *pound medium shrimp*
½   *pound medium scallops*
1   *pound swordfish, cut into 1½-inch square pieces*
1½ *cups basmati rice*
3   *tablespoons peanut oil*
2   *celery stalks, diced*
1   *onion, diced*
1   *red pepper, diced*
¼   *cup tequila*
    Ten Spices:
2   *garlic cloves, crushed*
1   *tablespoon ground coriander*
1   *tablespoon cumin*
1   *tablespoon oregano*
1   *tablespoon dried basil*
½   *tablespoon dried mustard*
2   *bay leaves*
2   *tablespoons capers*

3   *or more dashes Tabasco sauce*
¼   *cup lime juice*

Soak the raisins for 1 hour in fruit juice that has been warmed slightly.

Wash and pat dry all of the fish. Place the fish on four skewers alternating the shrimp, scallops, and swordfish. Set aside.

Prepare the rice according to the package instructions.

Heat the peanut oil in a large skillet with a cover on high heat. Add the celery, onion, and pepper. Turn heat down and sauté about 4 minutes. Add the 10 spices and sauté about 2 minutes more. Add the tequila and raisins with the juice. Sauté 1 more minute. Mix. Broil seafood skewers, turning every 2 to 3 minutes until done.

Place skewers on the rice, and spoon sauce over the skewers.

There are many different kinds of squash to choose from to make the following stew. I like to use the butternut variety because of the large amounts of beta-carotene found in it.

SQUASH AND CHICKEN STEW

serves 4

3   *chicken thighs*
2   *tablespoons olive oil*
1½   *cups cubed peeled butternut or other yellow flesh squash*
4 to 5   *small new potatoes, diced*
2   *large leeks, whites only, sliced*
4   *shallots, chopped*
1   *red bell pepper, cut into small strips*
5   *garlic cloves, mashed*
1   *large Granny Smith apple—cubed*
28   *ounces canned whole tomatoes, quartered, drained*

1   *cup mushrooms, sliced*
2   *teaspoons cinnamon*
    pinch of mace
5   *cloves*
    chopped cilantro or parsley
½   *cup chicken stock, canned or fresh*
    salt and pepper to taste

Preheat the oven to 325°. Put the chicken on a baking sheet and bake until done, about 40 to 50 minutes.

Remove the skin from the chicken, then remove the meat from the bones. Set aside.

In a large deep frying pan or Dutch oven, heat 2 tablespoons olive oil. Add the squash, potatoes, leeks, shallots, red bell pepper, garlic, and apple. Sauté about 10 minutes until the potatoes and squash are cooked through but still firm. Cook uncovered for 7 to 10 minutes for some liquid to evaporate. Add the tomatoes, mushrooms, chicken, cinnamon, mace, and cloves, and ½ cup chicken broth. Stir and let simmer 15 more minutes, add salt and pepper. Sprinkle with parsley or chopped cilantro.

The following recipe calls for many ingredients and quite a few cooking procedures. The good news is that this layer cake lasts for up to 10 days in the refrigerator and can feed up to 10 people in one seating.

If you have budget concerns, cut out the saffron. If you have cholesterol concerns, cut out the cheese and substitute a good thick tomato sauce (4 cups).

MEXICAN LAYER CAKE WITH FRESH SALSA

approximately 10 servings

2   zucchini, sliced thin
¾   pound string beans
1   pound mushrooms, sliced thin
2   celery stalks, sliced thin
1   16-ounce can corn kernels, drained
3   15-ounce cans black beans, drained
1   4-ounce can hot jalapeño chili peppers or ½ large fresh jalapeño, seeded
      and chopped (use rubber gloves) (you can roast the other half and
      use for the salsa)
7   Italian tomatoes, seeded and chopped
      salt and pepper to taste
9   large tortillas, flour or whole wheat
2   cups shredded jack cheese
2   cups shredded cheddar cheese
1   large bunch of cilantro, chopped
      sour cream (optional)
2   large sweet onions, chopped
2   tablespoons dried basil

SAUCE

3   cloves garlic, mashed
2   tablespoons dried oregano
1   tablespoon thyme
      good pinch of saffron threads
3   tablespoons olive oil
2   teaspoons salt
3   tablespoons chili powder
¾   cup chicken stock or water
2   carrots, sliced thin
1   tablespoon arrowroot mixed with 1 tablespoon water

To prepare the sauce: in a large skillet, sauté the garlic, oregano, thyme, and saffron in the olive oil. Add 2 teaspoons of salt. Add the chili powder and stir 2 to 3 more minutes. Add the chicken stock and arrowroot. Raise heat to thicken slightly. Turn off heat and set aside.

Slice and steam the carrots, zucchini, string beans, mushrooms, and celery. Do not overcook. Vegetables should remain crisp because they will be baked later on. Mash half of the black beans and mix into the rest of the whole beans. Place the steamed vegetables in a bowl and add the corn, black beans, jalapeño pepper, and tomatoes. Add salt and pepper to taste. Toss well.

Preheat the oven to 350°.

Grease a large baking dish or Mexican ceramic cooking bowl with butter or olive oil. Reheat the sauce slightly. Using a pastry brush, spread the sauce over a tortilla. Place the tortilla on the bottom of a 9 × 12-baking dish. Add a layer of vegetables, cheese, and cilantro. Place another tortilla on top and continue building the cake until all the ingredients are used up. Pour excess sauce on the top layer and add additional cheese. Bake 30 to 40 minutes. Remove from oven and let sit 5 minutes. Serve with salsa and fresh chopped cilantro and sour cream.

SALSA

(best if prepared one day ahead)

1   *small bunch fresh cilantro, chopped*
1   *four-ounce can hot jalapeño chili peppers, seeded and chopped or ½*
    large roasted jalapeño chili, seeded and chopped (use rubber gloves)
    (to roast jalapeño, blister skin under broiler; put in paper bag to
    steam; after 5 minutes, remove skin and seeds, and chop)
1   *5.5-ounce can tomato juice*
5   *Italian tomatoes, chopped and seeded*
2   *cloves garlic*
    juice of 1 lime
½   *of a medium sized sweet onion, chopped*
1   *small cucumber, skin removed and chopped*
    salt and pepper to taste

Blend the tomato juice and half of all the above ingredients in a food processor or blender. Pour the blended ingredients into a bowl with the rest of the chopped ingredients. The salsa should sit in the refrigerator at least 2 hours, or make it one day ahead.

Note about jalapeño peppers: some peppers are milder than others. Taste a very small amount on your tongue and add to the recipe according to your taste. Also please be careful not to touch these peppers. Do not put your hands near your eyes if you come in contact with them and wash the knife, cutting board, or any other surfaces after use with these peppers.

CORN CAKES WITH . . . ?

makes approximately 8 to 10 cakes

¾   cup yellow cornmeal
2   teaspoons brown sugar
1¼   cups milk
2   eggs, separate yolks from whites, keep both
    salt
    pinch white pepper
2   cloves of garlic, minced
1   cup corn kernels, preferably without sugar, drained
1   teaspoon salt
2   tablespoons butter or 1½ tablespoons olive oil

Combine the cornmeal, sugar, and milk in a saucepan. Bring the mixture to a boil over medium heat, stirring constantly for 5 minutes.

Remove the saucepan from the heat and let cool for 5 minutes. Stir in the egg yolks slowly. Add the salt, pepper, garlic, and corn kernels and mix well.

In a bowl, whip the egg whites with a pinch of salt until stiff. Stir in a quarter of the cornmeal mixture and then fold in the rest. Heat oil or butter in a nonstick skillet. Ladle out a small amount of batter. Brown on one side, then flip and cook the other side. Serve with pure maple syrup or top with any leftovers from the refrigerator. As a special treat, sauté shrimp or lobster. Put some shredded lettuce on each cake and top with fresh salsa, caviar, crème fraîche, shredded cheese, olives, etc. etc. etc.

This recipe was created from a leftover brown rice dish for a vegetarian friend of ours. We knew that rice would be enjoyed in this festive manner. This recipe can also be used to stuff peppers. Add some eggs and nuts and it would make a great vegetarian loaf.

STUFFED MUSHROOMS

serves 4

1   *cup wheat berries*
1   *cup short grain brown rice*
4   *cups water*
¼   *cup miso (soy bean paste)*
¼   *pound butter*
15 *or more large mushrooms, remove and chop stems*
1   *tablespoon canola oil*
½   *onion, chopped*
1   *red pepper, chopped*
1   *teaspoon dry basil*
½   *cup grated mozzarella cheese*
½   *cup Asiago cheese*
3   *tablespoons soy sauce*

To prepare the rice mixture, place the wheat berries, rice, water, miso, butter, and mushroom stems into a pot and bring to a boil. Simmer with the cover on for 1 hour. Wheat berries will remain slightly firm.

Heat canola oil in a skillet and sauté the onions and pepper with the basil and soy sauce until soft. Turn off the flame and let cool a few minutes. Add the rice and both cheeses and mix until it's dough-like and sticky.

Stuff the mushroom tops with the mixture and place them on a greased baking sheet. Bake at 350° for 30 minutes. Just before serving, place the mushrooms under the broiler for 1 minute to brown tops.

This was one of those spur of the moment soups. All of the ingredients were on hand as basic kitchen stocked goods. Ordinarily the sausages would not have been included as an ingredient, but because they just happened to be there, they were added to create just the right flavor.

WILD RICE AND BLACK BEAN SOUP

serves 6 to 8

4   quarts water
½   cup dry red wine
2   15-ounce cans black beans, drained
2   carrots, chopped
1   onion, chopped
1   rutabaga, chopped
3   celery stalks, chopped
2   Italian hot sausages, cooked and sliced
1   3-pound chicken, cut up, skin removed
3   tablespoons dry basil
1   tablespoon dry oregano
     soy sauce to taste
6   cloves garlic, mashed
2   tablespoons Dijon mustard
2   cups cooked wild rice
2   cups cooked brown rice

In a large pot add all the above except the rice. Simmer ¾ of an hour. Then add the rice and simmer an additional 15 minutes. Let stand ½ to 1 hour. Reheat before serving.

COLD MARINATED VEGETABLE SALAD

serves 4

VEGETABLES

1	*pound broccoli, diced*
1	*zucchini, diced*
3	*shitake mushrooms, chopped (fresh)*
1	*red pepper, chopped*
10	*green olives, sliced*
½	*red onion, diced*
½	*cup frozen peas, thawed*

MARINADE

½	*cup canola oil*
¼	*cup white wine*
½	*cup lemon juice*
3	*tablespoons chopped fresh basil*
	black pepper to taste
1	*teaspoon dried sage*
2	*cloves garlic, mashed*
2	*tablespoons mayonnaise*
2	*tablespoons hot sesame oil*

Steam the broccoli and zucchini until just done. Do not overcook. Combine all the vegetables.

Mix together all ingredients for the marinade, pour over the vegetables, stir, and cover. Place in the refrigerator overnight.

AROMATIC GREEN SAUCE FOR STEAMED VEGETABLES

1   *12-ounce package chopped frozen spinach, defrosted, juice removed and reserved*
4   *scallions, chopped*
6   *large garlic cloves, mashed*
1   *large bunch of fresh basil, stems removed*
2   *tablespoons vegetable oil*
    soy sauce to taste

Rinse and drain the spinach in a colander, reserving the liquid. Sauté the spinach in the oil until slightly tender. Add the scallions, garlic, and basil. Sauté until soft, keeping this mixture moist by adding soy sauce and spinach liquid. Transfer to a food processor. Puree until it becomes a pouring consistency.

The following recipe enhances fish which has previously been frozen. The sauce adds a zip to fish which has lost some of its fresh flavor in the freezing process.

CURRIED HALIBUT SALAD

serves 4

2½ *pounds fresh or frozen halibut*
1   *onion, chopped*
1   *tablespoon curry powder*
4   *tablespoons canola or peanut oil*
2   *tablespoons water*
2   *3-ounce cans sliced black olives*
3   *tablespoons capers*
5   *tablespoons mayonnaise*
2   *celery stalks, chopped finely*

Cook the halibut in the oven at 350° for 20 minutes until done.

Sauté the onions and curry powder in the oil over low heat. Add the water to create a sauce. Cover and cook for 3 minutes until onions are soft. Let cool. Add capers, celery, mayonnaise and cooked halibut. Mix. Refrigerate until cold, about 3 hours.

This soup was originated as a first course for a cold February evening dinner party. A hearty soup without meat was required because lamb was being served as the entree.

LEEK AND BARLEY SOUP

serves 4 to 6

3 *large leeks, washed*
2 *tablespoons dry tarragon*
2 *tablespoons winter savory*
1 *tablespoon fresh dill*
2 *tablespoons vegetable oil*
2 *stalks celery, diced*
1 *can beer*
½ *cup tomato sauce*
½ *cup salsa*
2 *quarts water*
4 *cups chicken stock*
1 *cup barley (not cooked)*
   salt to taste
10 *pea pods, cut up*

Sauté the leeks, tarragon, winter savory, and dill in the oil in the bottom of large soup pot. Add all the remaining ingredients except the pea pods and simmer for 1 hour. Add the pea pods and let stand for ½ hour. Serve.

The idea for this pie came from a Spanish cookbook. It has changed and evolved over the years. The last addition was the brie.

SPINACH PIE WITH BRIE

serves 4 to 6

PIE CRUST

1   cup whole wheat flour
1   cup enriched white flour
1   tablespoon curry powder
½   teaspoon salt
4   ounces butter, sliced
8   ounces very cold cream cheese, cut in cubes
¼   cup ice water

FILLING

1   teaspoon dried rosemary
1   teaspoon dried basil
4   garlic cloves, mashed
1   onion, chopped
8   mushrooms, chopped
3   tablespoons vegetable oil
2   12-ounce packages frozen spinach, rinsed and drained
½   cup bread crumbs
½   cup Parmesan cheese
1   cup grated Fontina, cheddar, or Swiss cheese
4   hard-boiled eggs, chopped
½   cup tomato sauce
2   eggs
½   pound French brie, rind removed and cut into pieces

To make the crust: in a food processor (because this crust is special, a food processor must be used rather than a blender or mixer), add the flours, curry powder, salt, butter, and cream cheese. Slowly add water until dough forms a ball. Cut the ball in half. Form them into 2 flat 5″ diameter circles. Wrap them in plastic wrap and refrigerate 1 hour. Roll both out separately on a lightly floured surface. Place one in a 10-inch pie tin. Save the other for the top.

To make the filling: in a large skillet, add the vegetable oil, sauté the rosemary, basil, garlic, onion, and mushrooms in the oil. Cover and cook until soft. Mix in the spinach. Turn off flame and mix together with the remainder of the ingredients except the brie. Place the brie on the bottom pie crust. Cover with the spinach mixture. Place the rest of the dough on top. Join the top and bottom by squeezing them together along the side of the tin. Puncture with a few fork holes. Bake 1 hour at 350°.

BASIC MEAT AND POULTRY STOCK

To make any stock, you must simmer together a combination of spices, bones, and meat, or just vegetables. It's easy, but the commitment ranges from 3 to 4 hours. This is because the liquid reduces and the flavor becomes concentrated. You can also gather bones and scraps of meat leftover from other recipes, freeze them, and when a sufficient amount (say 3 to 4 pounds) has been reached, pull them out and begin. Some helpful hints: for meat and chicken, the liquid should simmer, not boil. This keeps the fat mainly on top and not in the body of the stock. Skimming the surface is a must to get rid of two unwanted substances, the fat and the froth.

makes about 2 to 3 quarts

2½ *pounds of beef or chicken bones and their trimmings*
2 *carrots, cut in large pieces*
3 *celery stalks, cut in large pieces*
3 *whole garlic cloves*
1 *teaspoon dried thyme*
4 *parsley sprigs*
3 *whole cloves*
2 *large onions, sliced*
3 *quarts cold water*
2½ *teaspoons salt*

Place all the ingredients in a 6 to 8-quart stockpot, set over medium heat. As liquid starts to simmer, skim off the froth. Let it simmer 3 to 4 hours. Continue skimming throughout. Add some boiling water if the liquid evaporates below the level of the ingredients. Spoon off the fat as it rises to the top. Strain and press the solids through a sieve or double cheese cloth. The stock may be frozen.

FISH STOCK

2½   *pounds bones and trimmings from any nonoily white fish (such as halibut, flounder, sole or whiting. Shrimp and lobster shells are also good.) Makes about 3½ cups of stock.*

10   *parsley sprigs (no leaves as they tend to darken the stock)*

1   *large onion, sliced*

2   *tablespoons fresh lemon juice*

1   *teaspoon salt*

1   *cup dry white wine or water*

4   *cups cold water*

In a large stockpot, bring all of the above ingredients to a boil. Lower the heat to simmer. Leave uncovered for 1 hour, skimming the froth from the surface. Strain the stock through a fine sieve or double cheese cloth by pressing down on the solids. Let cool completely. Stock may be kept chilled in the refrigerator for one week if it is brought to boil every two days to keep from spoiling.

VEGETABLE STOCK

Use the basic recipe for the meat stock, but substitute vegetables for the meat. Use any variety you wish, making sure you use about 2½ pounds of vegetables, cut coarsely. Include carrots and celery in this amount. Add extra spices like cinnamon sticks (2) or crushed cardamon seed (1 teaspoon) to add extra flavor for Indian-style soups. Add leeks (white part only), but stay away from cabbage and cauliflower as they tend to have a very strong flavor. Makes about 4 cups of stock.

SPICED BAKED SWORDFISH

serves 4

½   teaspoon ground red pepper flakes
2   cloves garlic, mashed
1   teaspoon ground black pepper
4 to 6   ounces swordfish fillets, or any firm-fleshed fish, such as halibut,
        shark, trout, or even salmon
⅓   cup butter or olive oil
2   tablespoons low-sodium soy sauce
4   tablespoons lime juice
1   teaspoon salt

In a small bowl, combine the red pepper flakes, salt, garlic, and black pepper.

Preheat the oven to 400°. Place the fish in a greased baking dish and rub the spice mixture onto the fish. Combine the butter or olive oil, soy sauce, and lime juice and pour over the fish.

Bake the fish approximately 15 minutes. Pour extra sauce from the baking dish over the fish. Serve with fluffy hot rice.

APRICOT COUSCOUS WITH SMOKED MEATS

serves 4

1 cup chicken stock or 1 cup water
1 cup couscous
½ cup dried apricots soaked in very hot water for 30 minutes. Drain, cut
     in quarters.
½ pound smoked ham, chicken, or turkey, cut in thin strips
     approximately 1½ inches long
½ small red sweet onion, chopped
¼ cup (packed) chopped parsley
1 tablespoon olive oil
   ground fresh pepper

Bring the chicken broth or water to a boil and add the couscous. Turn the heat off and cover. Let stand for 5 minutes, then fluff with a fork. In a medium bowl, toss the apricots, meat, onion, and parsley together. Drizzle the olive oil over the mixture. Spoon the meat mixture over the couscous. Stir to mix. Add pepper to taste. Serve as a side dish or spoon over crisp lettuce leaves.

Serve this bread with any good curry dip or just some melted butter and garlic or sprinkle with grated cheese and parsley.

POORI—INDIAN BREAD

2   *cups whole wheat flour*
2   *teaspoons baking powder*
3½   *tablespoons peanut oil*
1   *cup cold water*

In a large bowl, combine the flour, baking powder, 2½ tablespoons peanut oil, and water. Roll dough into 1- to 2-inch balls. Refrigerate for 1 hour.

Heat 1 tablespoon peanut oil in a nonstick skillet. Roll out each ball into a ⅛-inch thick circle. Drop in the hot skillet, patting it down with a spatula until bubbly and puffy; turn once. Drain on paper towels.

POACHED SOLE WITH ROCK SHRIMP SAUCE

serves 4

1½ to 2   *pounds sole fillets*
1   *small onion, chopped*
2   *scallions, chopped*
½   *cup white wine*
½   *cup bottled clam juice or fish stock*
1   *teaspoon salt*
1   *teaspoon black pepper*

Preheat the oven to 350°. Put the fillets in buttered baking dish, overlap if necessary. Sprinkle the onion, salt, pepper, and scallions over the fish.

In a small glass bowl, mix together the wine and clam juice. Pour the liquid over the fish to barely cover. Place the dish in the bottom third of the oven. Bake 7 to 12 minutes or until the fish is cooked through. Do not overcook. Drain the liquid from the dish, for use in the shrimp sauce. Return the fish to oven, keeping warm at 350°.

ROCK SHRIMP SAUCE

¾ pound rock shrimp or, if not available, 8 medium-size shrimp
1 cup poaching liquid (from above recipe)
2 tablespoons butter
½ cup heavy cream
1 to 2 tablespoons lemon juice
2 teaspoons Hungarian paprika (hot)
salt and pepper to taste

Wash, devein, and remove the shells from the shrimp. Cut the shrimp into small pieces and heat 1 tablespoon butter in a small skillet, add shrimp and sauté until the shrimp turns bright pink, approximately 2 to 3 minutes. Remove the shrimp and add the poaching liquid, butter, cream, and lemon juice to the liquid already in the pan. Heat until the sauce thickens slightly. Return the shrimp to the pan to heat through.

Pour the sauce over the fillets, sprinkle with paprika, salt, and pepper to taste.

CHICKEN WITH ROASTED HERBS

serves 4

1	*4- to 5-pound chicken*
3	*garlic cloves, cut in half*
1	*lime*
1	*medium onion, quartered and sprinkled with salt and pepper*
1	*tablespoon dried tarragon*
1	*tablespoon dried thyme*
3	*tablespoons salt*
1	*tablespoon dried sage*
1	*tablespoon dried oregano*
1	*tablespoon dried caraway seeds*
3	*tablespoons lemon juice*
3	*tablespoons wine vinegar*
4	*tablespoons olive oil*
	fresh pepper
1½	*tablespoons dried dill*
1	*tablespoon cinnamon*

Preheat the oven to 475°.

Put the chicken in a large roasting pan. Rub the garlic over the skin (do not discard). Cut the lime in half and stuff the lime and onion into the cavity.

In a blender, combine the garlic cloves, tarragon, thyme, salt, sage, dill, cinnamon, oregano, caraway seeds, lemon juice, and vinegar and blend until a paste is formed. Put ⅓ of the paste in the chicken cavity. Tie the legs together with the kitchen string to close the cavity. Put the olive oil in the remaining paste. Coat the chicken thoroughly with the paste. Grind fresh pepper over chicken.

Put the pan on the middle rack in the oven. Roast for 30 minutes. Reduce heat to 350° for approximately 45 minutes. Baste 3 to 4 times during this cooking period. When done (the juices will run clear), remove the chicken from the oven. Let stand for 10 minutes before carving.

LEEKS AND EGGPLANT WITH HOT MUSTARD SAUCE

serves 4

1   *large eggplant*
2   *large leeks, white parts only*
3   *tablespoons Dijon mustard*
2   *tablespoons minced fresh herbs (basil, thyme, oregano, tarragon)*
1   *tablespoon fruit juice of any kind*
1   *tablespoon wine vinegar*
⅓   *cup olive oil*
1   *tablespoon butter*
⅓   *cup chicken stock or water*
    salt and pepper
    pinch red pepper flakes

Preheat the oven to 325°.

Peel and cut the eggplant into thin slices and salt both sides. Put the slices in a colander for juices to drain. Slice the leeks lengthwise and rinse. Remove dirt from inner leaves.

In a small bowl, whisk together the mustard, red pepper flakes, and ⅓ cup olive oil until creamy. Add the herbs, vinegar, and fruit juice and whisk again. Let stand at room temperature at least 10 minutes.

Alternate layers of eggplant and leeks in a buttered baking dish. Drizzle ⅓ cup olive oil and melted butter over the vegetables. Add the chicken stock or water. Bake for 30 minutes or until the water has evaporated. Remove the vegetables to a warm serving dish. Spoon the sauce on top.

COD SALAD

serves 4 as an appetizer or side dish

¾ pound salt cod,* soaked overnight in water
½ cup toasted pecans
½ cup toasted bread crumbs, not seasoned
¾ pound fresh water chestnuts
1 8½-ounce can whole cranberries, rinsed and drained (you can choose a
     different fruit, such as diced pineapple, if you find cranberries mushy)
1 large bunch arugula, chopped
   chopped fresh chives

DRESSING

¾ cup olives, pitted
¼ cup olive oil
1 teaspoon salt
2 tablespoons rice vinegar

Place the olives, olive oil, and salt in a blender or food processor. Add the rice vinegar and mix well.

Drain and wash the cod. Pat dry and cut into strips.

Preheat oven to 350°. Put the pecans on a cookie sheet and bake 5 to 7 minutes. Put the bread crumbs on a separate cookie sheet and bake until toasted. With a sharp knife, remove the skin from the chestnuts. Rinse under cold water. Slice the chestnuts.

Place the cod, chestnuts, and cranberries into a bowl and pour the olive sauce over. Toss well. Place the chopped arugula on chilled salad plates and top with the cod mixture. Sprinkle the toasted bread crumbs, pecans, and chives on top.

---

*Available in Italian specialty stores or seafood markets.

For this recipe you can use the quick cooking polenta (5 to 10 minutes) or, if you need upper body work, purchase the 30-minute-constant-stirring brand and build those muscles. We can't tell the difference in taste, let us know if you can.

POLENTA WITH SAUSAGE RAGOUT

serves 4

½ *pound polenta*
½ *cup pine nuts*
3 *tablespoons olive oil*
4 *sausages, your choice (but not breakfast or frozen; hot Italian or turkey or lamb work best)*
1 *small onion, chopped*
2 *cloves garlic, mashed*
2 *cups jarred marinara sauce or your own homemade*
2 *teaspoons sugar*
    pinch red pepper flakes
½ *cup beer or wine*
1 *small bunch fresh basil leaves, chopped*
    salt and pepper to taste

Prepare the polenta according to the package directions.* Let cool completely or refrigerate at least 2 hours. Before browning, the polenta must be at room temperature.

In a preheated 350° oven, lightly toast the pine nuts for 5 minutes.

In a nonstick frying pan, add 1 tablespoon of olive oil and brown the sausages. Remove from pan and drain on paper towels. Cut the sausages into 1-inch pieces. Remove the grease from the pan. Add the onion and

---

*Pour the polenta into a greased shallow baking dish, approximately 1-inch deep, using a spatula to spread evenly. Polenta should be about ¾-inch thick.

sauté until tender. Add the garlic, tomato sauce, sugar, red pepper flakes, beer or wine, and basil. Simmer 20 minutes. Return the sausages to the pan and cook 10 minutes more. Salt and pepper to taste.

Cut the polenta into squares. Heat a skillet and add the additional 2 tablespoons of olive oil. Brown the polenta on both sides. Remove from the skillet and top with a heaping spoonful of the sausage mixture and sprinkle pine nuts on top.

PENNE WITH BLUE CHEESE, SPINACH, AND TOMATOES

serves 4

  5 tablespoons olive oil
  4 shallots, chopped
  7 Italian tomatoes, chopped and seeded
  5 cloves garlic, mashed
     salt and pepper to taste
  ½ cup white wine
  1 bunch fresh spinach leaves, washed, patted dry, and chopped
  ¾ cup chopped fresh basil
  7 ounces good blue cheese
  1 pound penne pasta
  ½ cup grated Asiago or Romano cheese
     a couple of sprigs of parsley, chopped

In a large skillet, heat the olive oil over medium heat. Add the shallots and stir until wilted. Add the tomatoes, garlic, salt, pepper, and wine, and simmer 10 to 15 minutes. Add the spinach and basil and stir another 2 to 3 minutes. Using the edge of a wooden spoon, mash the blue cheese into the mixture until melted and the sauce thickens.

Cook the pasta according to the package directions. Drain the pasta. Add to the skillet with the sauce and reheat gently. Sprinkle with Asiago or Romano cheese. Top with some fresh parsley and serve.

Pistachios have a unique flavor and are delicious when coupled with other ingredients, especially root vegetables. You can substitute any vegetable for the green beans and choose any crisp salad green to go with it.

PISTACHIO VEGETABLE SALAD

serves 4

1	*ounce dried mushrooms*
1	*large fennel bulb, trimmed, thinly sliced*
2 to 5	*shallots, chopped*
1	*tablespoon olive oil*
½	*pound red potatoes*
½	*pound green beans, trimmed and cut into 2-inch pieces*
½	*pound turnips, sliced*
1	*cup pistachios, shelled*
	assortment of fresh salad greens

DRESSING

½	*cup olive oil*
¼	*cup red wine vinegar*
2	*tablespoons Dijon style mustard*
¼	*cup mayonnaise*
¼	*cup sour cream or yogurt*
2	*tablespoons chopped fresh dill or 2 teaspoons dried dill*

Soak the mushrooms in hot water for 30 minutes. Rinse and pat dry and cut in half. In a small frying pan, sauté the fennel and shallots in 1 tablespoon olive oil.

Boil the potatoes in salted water approximately 10 to 15 minutes until just tender, then slice. Stir together the potatoes, green beans, turnips, mushrooms, pistachios, and onion-fennel mixture in a large bowl. Salt and pepper to taste.

In a blender, or by hand, mix all the dressing ingredients together. Pour over the vegetables. Serve warm or chilled over the salad greens.

CHERRY BERRY NUT STEW

serves 4 to 6

1	cup flour
2½	pounds beef for stew, cut up into 1- to 2-inch squares
3	tablespoons peanut oil or nonflavored oil
2	teaspoons salt
1½	cups sherry
2	cups beef broth, fresh or canned
8	Italian tomatoes, sliced
1	tablespoon Hungarian paprika (hot)
1	large onion, chopped
2	bay leaves
4	cloves garlic, mashed
2	teaspoons black peppercorns, coarsely ground
¾	pound seedless grapes
3	carrots, sliced
2	celery stalks sliced into 1-inch pieces
1	6- to 8- ounce package dried pitted cherries
2	tablespoons honey
¾	cup chopped toasted nuts

Put the flour into a plastic bag. Add the beef and toss and coat well. Remove the meat from the bag—leave remaining flour in the bag. Heat oil in a large nonstick skillet or Dutch oven. Add the meat and brown well on all sides. Sprinkle a small amount of salt over the meat. Remove the meat from the pan. Pour the sherry in and deglaze, making sure you remove all the brown bits from the bottom of the pan. Reduce the liquid by half. This should take approximately 7 to 10 minutes. Lower the heat. Add the beef broth, tomatoes, paprika, onion, and bay leaves, and cook another 5 minutes.

Preheat the oven to 350°. Put the meat and tomato mixture into a heavy baking dish or stockpot. Stir in the garlic and black pepper. Bake 45 minutes.

Remove approximately ¾ cup of liquid from the stew. Put in a bowl and whisk in 2 tablespoons of flour from the bag. Pour the flour mixture back into the pot and stir well. Bake another 30 minutes. Check the seasonings.

Add the grapes, carrots, celery, cherries, and honey to the pot. Stir and cook 10 more minutes. Check the meat to see if it is tender. If not, bake another 10 to 15 minutes. Remove the bay leaves. Let stand. If not serving immediately, let cool before refrigerating. Stew usually tastes better the second day, so plan ahead if possible. Before serving, sprinkle with nuts. Serve over rice, noodles, couscous.

SQUASH AND SEAFOOD SOUP

serves 4

1   *butternut squash*
1   *large ear fresh corn, husked*
1   *medium onion, chopped*
2   *cloves garlic, mashed*
3   *tablespoons butter*
1   *cup clam broth, or frozen fish stock (see recipe on page 153)*
4   *cups chicken stock*
½   *pound medium-large shrimp*
⅓   *pound firm-fleshed fish (swordfish, shark, or tuna)*
½   *pound lump crabmeat*
2   *teaspoons nutmeg*
   salt and pepper to taste
¼   *cup chopped parsley*
4   *lemon slices, used as decoration*

Cut the squash into quarters and scoop out the seeds. Put the squash and corn into a steamer and steam 10 to 15 minutes until vegetables are tender. Cool.

While the corn and squash cool, sauté the chopped onion and garlic in 2 tablespoons of butter, about 2 minutes.

Puree the squash in a blender or food processor with the clam broth or fish stock and 1 cup of chicken stock. Add the onion-butter mixture and puree 1 more minute. Pour the squash mixture into a soup pot. With a sharp knife, remove the corn from the cob, pressing down hard on the cob to release the corn milk. Add the corn to the pot. Add the remaining 3 cups of chicken stock and simmer.

Clean and devein the shrimp. Cut the fish into small chunks. In a medium saucepan, melt 1 tablespoon of butter and sauté the fish and parsley. When the fish is fairly well cooked, add the shrimp, crabmeat, and nutmeg. Do not overcook the shrimp. Add some chicken broth if needed to cook the fish. Salt and pepper to taste.

Pour the squash soup into heated soup bowls. Put a generous scoop of fish in the center of each bowl. Top with a lemon slice and a sprinkling of parsley.

TURKEY HASH

If you have time and energy, this can be made with a fresh turkey breast, fresh chicken, or any leftover chicken or meat.

serves 4

1	*pound cooked turkey or chicken, shredded or cubed (if using fresh cooked meat, let cool before cutting up)*
4 to 5	*small new potatoes*
3	*tablespoons olive oil*
1	*small onion, chopped*
4 to 5	*shallots, chopped*
1	*celery stalk, sliced*
1	*green bell pepper, chopped*
2	*cloves garlic, mashed or put through a garlic press*
½	*cup chopped parsley*
1	*tablespoon hot Hungarian paprika*
½	*cup unseasoned bread crumbs*
½	*cup raisins or currants*
¾	*cup pecans, slightly toasted*
	salt and pepper to taste
2	*eggs, beaten*

Chop the meat into small pieces.

Steam or boil the potatoes until just done—do not overcook. Dice.

Heat the olive oil in a large frying pan over medium-low heat. Add the onion, shallots, celery, and bell pepper and sauté 4 to 5 minutes. Turn off the heat and stir in the garlic, parsley, paprika, and potatoes. Transfer to a large mixing bowl and add the meat, bread crumbs, raisins, pecans, and salt and pepper to taste.

Add the beaten eggs and blend well with the other ingredients. Pour the meat mixture into a frying pan and brown on all sides over medium-high heat.

Serve over rice, fresh shredded lettuce, pasta, beans, or whatever grabs you that day. Also top with a fried egg and crumbled bacon for a real treat.

SWEET AND SOUR NOODLE STIR FRY

serves 4

1 medium-sized carrot, cut in small strips (julienne)
2 cups shredded cabbage
¾ pound rice noodles or angel hair pasta
1 small onion, sliced thinly
1 small firm pear, diced
   juice of ½ lemon, sprinkled over diced pear
2 tablespoons peanut oil
3 tablespoons red wine vinegar
2 tablespoons honey
2 teaspoons salt
2 medium tomatoes, chopped and seeded
¼ cup white sesame seeds
¼ cup black sesame seeds
1 scallion, sliced thinly
2 teaspoons ground cumin

Steam the carrots and cabbage gently for 2 to 3 minutes. They should remain crisp.

Prepare the noodles according to the package directions. Do not overcook. Rinse the noodles in cold water, drain very well. Put some peanut oil on your fingers and toss the pasta, separating the pieces. Lay the pasta out on a cutting surface and cut into 3-inch pieces.

To prepare the sweet-and-sour sauce: sauté the onion and pear in 1 tablespoon of the peanut oil in a small frying pan for two minutes. Add the vinegar, honey, salt, and cumin and cook 5 minutes more.

Heat the remaining oil in a wok and toss in the noodles, carrots, cabbage, and tomatoes and stir fry for 1 to 2 minutes. Remove from heat and stir in the sweet-and-sour sauce.

Serve immediately—sprinkling each plate with sesame seeds and scallions.

Anyone addicted to pesto should think about visiting Camogli next time the travel bug strikes. Just 20 kilometers from Portofino, this little town on a cliff served up one of the simplest pesto dishes we ever tasted.

CAMOGLI LASAGNA

serves 4

⅓   *cup olive oil*
¼   *cup pignoli nuts*
2   *cloves garlic*
1   *large bunch basil leaves, chopped*
⅓   *cup heavy cream*
½   *cup chicken or vegetable broth*
4   *fresh lasagna pasta sheets, or ½ box dried lasagna noodles*
4 to 5   *anchovies, cut into ½" pieces*
1   *pound fresh baby spinach leaves, stemmed, washed, and patted dry,*
        or 2 10-ounce packages frozen spinach
     thin slices of Pecorino or Parmesan cheese
½   *cup Asiago cheese (leave ¼ cup for topping)*

To prepare the pesto sauce: put the oil, pignolis, garlic, Asiago cheese, basil, cream, and broth into a blender or food processor and puree. Add more broth if necessary.

In a large pot of rapidly boiling water, cook the lasagna pasta. Do not overcook. Drain the sheets in a colander. Put a small amount of olive oil on the sheets to keep them from sticking.

Spread 1 tablespoon of the pesto sauce on the bottom of a shallow cooking pan—not larger than 9 × 12 inches. Add one layer of pasta. Place 2 anchovies, some spinach leaves, cheese slices, and some more pesto sauce over the pasta sheet. Continue layering the lasagna until all the ingredients are used up. Sprinkle the top layer with some Asiago cheese.

Preheat oven at 350°. Bake for 10 minutes. Serve immediately. Top with extra cheese.

On a cold fall afternoon in Barcelona, we entered a restaurant with no menu to be seen, but crowds galore were hanging around waiting to be seated. Once at the table, we ordered the soup. What emerged was good, but as each mouthful went down, we wished the chef had added just a little garlic and saffron. Once we got back to the States, we tried our own version.

SOUP CASTELLANO

serves 4

1   *large onion, chopped*
3   *tablespoons olive oil*
6   *cloves garlic*
    salt and pepper to taste
    a hearty pinch of saffron (oh, go ahead and splurge on this delectable,
        beautiful, unique herb)
8   *cups rich chicken or vegetable stock**
1   *large egg, beaten*
2   *cups cubed sourdough or French bread*
    chopped parsley
6   *ripe tomatoes, seeded and chopped*

Sauté the onion in the olive oil over medium heat until wilted, not browned. Stir in the garlic, tomatoes, salt, and pepper to taste. Sauté 5 more minutes.

Put the broth and saffron into a stockpot and simmer over medium heat for half an hour. Check the seasonings. Add the garlic-tomato-onion mixture and simmer 5 more minutes. Add the beaten egg and stir.

Remove from heat. Add the bread cubes and top with some fresh parsley. Serve immediately.

---

*We usually allow for substituting canned broth, but for this soup it's important to make your own rich stock. See the Basic Chicken and Vegetable Stocks on page 87.

The next recipe is a good one for getting rid of all the leftovers that won't last another day. Use any pasta, leftover, fresh, or dry.

PASTA PANCAKE

serves 2 to 3

½ to 1   *pound pasta*
   1   *cup chopped vegetables, fresh plus any day-old will do. If you don't have leftovers, use an assortment of chopped celery, beans, zucchini, etc.*
   ½   *cup chopped nuts*
   1   *cup grated cheese or soy cheese plus ¼ cup for topping salt and pepper to taste*
   2   *eggs or 1 egg and 1 egg white*
   2   *tablespoons olive oil*
   3   *scallions, sliced thin*
   ¼   *cup black or white sesame seeds hot chili sesame oil (optional)*
   ½   *cup chopped meat*
   1   *tablespoon any fresh chopped herbs or 3 teaspoons dried*

Prepare the pasta according to the package directions.

If using fresh, chopped vegetables, steam them but do not overcook.

In a large mixing bowl, put the pasta, vegetables, meat, herbs, nuts, cheese, salt, and pepper. Beat the eggs and stir them into the mixture. Let sit for 10 minutes.

In a large, nonstick frying pan, heat the olive oil. The pan should be hot but not smoking. Pour in the mixture, creating two separate pancakes. When one side is light brown and crispy, flip over and cook the other side. Flatten the mixture down with a spatula. Remove pancakes from the pan. Sprinkle with remaining cheese, sliced scallions, and sesame seeds. Drizzle the sesame seed oil over each pancake. Serve immediately.

SWEET-AND-SOUR CABBAGE WITH HERBED SPAETZLE

This recipe is for someone who has a little more time for preparation. The cabbage needs to bake for at least 1 hour, and although the dumplings are easy to make, the batter must rest at room temperature for at least 40 minutes. For pure vegetarians, omit the chicken stock and use either water or fruit juice. Dried herbs can be substituted for fresh. Plan on using at least 2 tablespoons chopped fresh, or 2 teaspoons dried for each herb you choose.

serves 4

1   *large red cabbage, sliced*
1   *cup chicken stock*
½   *cup red wine vinegar plus 2 tablespoons*
½   *cup honey*
2   *teaspoons salt*
2   *teaspoons caraway seeds*
¾   *cup white raisins (optional)*
    a couple of good grinds of fresh black pepper

Preheat oven to 350°.

In a heavy baking dish, combine all of the above ingredients. Bake for at least 1 hour. Stir mixture every 15 minutes to keep cabbage coated. Liquid will evaporate slowly as the cabbage shrinks in size. If cabbage is not getting soft, add more liquid until most of it is absorbed.

SPAETZLE

1½   *cups flour*

3   *eggs*

⅓   *cup semolina flour*

3   *tablespoons fresh chopped chives, dill, basil (any fresh herbs are good)*

⅓   *cup ricotta cheese*

1   *teaspoon ground nutmeg*

1   *teaspoon salt*

1   *large onion, sliced*

1   *tablespoon olive oil*

½   *cup water, adding more if needed until batter is well blended*

In a large bowl, combine all of the above ingredients except the water, oil, and onion. Add the water slowly and mix with an electric mixer until the batter is thick, adding more water if mixture is too thick. Let sit at room temperature for 40 minutes.

To cook spaetzle: bring a large pot of water to boil and add 1 to 2 teaspoons salt. With a small spoon, scoop rounds of dough and drop them into the water. Dumplings will rise to the top when done. Remove with a slotted spoon.

In a large, nonstick frying pan, add the olive oil and sauté the onion until golden brown. Add the spaetzle in small batches and sauté in the same pan 2–3 minutes.

Remove the cabbage from the oven. There should be no liquid left in the dish. If there is, cook longer at 375°. Remove from the oven and serve with the onions and spaetzle.

DINNER AT EIGHT: THE CREATION OF A MEAL

"I like reality. It tastes of bread."

—JEAN ANOUILH

EVERY MEAL PROVIDES THE OPPORTUNITY FOR THE COOK TO CREATE. IT IS UP TO the cook to grab the moment and make it happen. *The Zen of Cooking* has been about this process and we invite you to join us as we create a dinner that will provide joy for us during its preparation and pleasure for our guests when it's eaten.

There is no doubt that it is a special dinner. And although it is not black tie, it is important. It is a celebratory dinner for us and our friends and family. We have finished the book! This is a moment to look back, a moment to go forward, and a time to see, taste, smell, touch, and listen.

The dinner begins back where we started—in the kitchen discussing with enthusiasm the peanut butter pasta and the feast we are going to prepare.

> LUCILLE: "You're not thinking of using this dish in our formal meal, are you?"
>
> CLAIRE: "Why not? What's wrong with cold peanut butter noodles?"
>
> LUCILLE: "It's too every day. This is a formal meal."
>
> CLAIRE: "Okay, okay, pasta *and* spinach rolls."

LUCILLE: "All right. Peanut butter pasta, spinach rolls, and some barbecued eggplant on the pasta. Barbecued eggplant is hot in Milan. Maybe we can claim it's 'Tuscan.' We could barbecue some Tuscan onions, mushrooms, and red peppers at the same time as the eggplant and use them later in the meal. And then serve Stuffed Lamb."

CLAIRE: "Too heavy, way too heavy."

LUCILLE: "Yeah, I guess you're right. Too heavy with the pasta and the stuffed spinach."

CLAIRE: "Not stuffed spinach. The spinach is just steamed, pressed, rolled in a tamari sauce, and covered lightly with cracker crumbs and sesame seeds. It's not heavy at all."

LUCILLE: "Cracker crumbs sounds like too much. Just use the sesame seeds."

Eventually we decided that the cold spinach rolls would provide color, flavor, and, by virtue of the time it would take to prepare each roll, a very hands-on preparation experience we would enjoy.

At first Claire wanted a fish appetizer, preferably ceviche. After Lucille rejected that notion we finally agreed on ramekins filled with hot curried shrimps, scallops, and a firm fish (like mahi-mahi, or whatever was fresh the day of the meal), accented with a crispy mashed potato crust.

And the meal was unfolding. Three appetizers: Barbecued Eggplant over spicy Peanut Butter Pasta; cold Sesame Spinach Rolls wrapped in scallion slivers; and hot Curried Seafood. We stepped back to take a look at what we had. From one perspective, yellows, greens, and white. From another, soft, crunchy, and crispy. From yet another, we fused Italian and Chinese influence with the Tuscan pasta and the Oriental-like spinach rolls.

But what about the salad?

LUCILLE: "Let's do something American."

CLAIRE: "For instance . . ."

LUCILLE: "A salad you can get your teeth into—no designer leaves and nothing diced."

Somehow the creative process progressed. Out of these first notions and concerns over spiciness, brightness, and lightness emerged a transitional course: Very cold mango slices with a dollop of fresh mint sauce that would clear the palate and prepare for the main courses.

A large American-style salad before the main course would be filled with chunks of tomatoes, peppers, raw carrots, peas, fresh basil, and celery. A tarragon or blue cheese dressing would accompany it, depending on the flavor of the main dish.

LUCILLE: "Maybe stuffed chicken breasts would be a good choice."

CLAIRE: "Stuffed with what? I think we ought to have something elegant and light. Let's keep it to a salad and . . . something clean like turkey or chicken breasts marinated with jalapeño peppers and tomatoes."

LUCILLE: "Maybe Rock Cornish game hens with some interesting breads—rosemary or olive—but I don't know about chicken or turkey. I want some meat that stands on its own."

CLAIRE: "We've got to coordinate the spiciness of the meat, breads, and salad dressing. How about veal?"

LUCILLE: "Let me think . . . a stuffed veal roll with a tangy cilantro pepper sauce."

CLAIRE: "Yeah, maybe stuffed isn't such a bad idea after all. We'll call it a veal rollette and serve it with the barbecued vegetables, but let's keep the breads simple. We have plenty of different flavors in the other dishes."

We agreed on a veal rollette consisting of thinly sliced veal wrapped around highly seasoned chopped veal, jellyroll style, and basted in a hot pepper and cilantro sauce. This would be augmented with the barbecued mushrooms, onions, and red peppers. We would buy three breads from our favorite bakery: a large flat onion focaccia, potato and rosemary, and a hearty sourdough.

Between the conception and actual eating of the meal are the makings of a road well traveled. In this special case, we had decided to pave it with diamonds. We had already indulged our free-floating creativity in the appetizer and entree choices, and we would put no limit on the time, energy, and money to pull it off.

This would mean taking the time to go to as many specialty shops as the ingredients demanded and our hearts desired. We would get the seafood the day of the meal, but we would need a few days of running around town before the actual preparation.

The pasta shop led to a selection of fresh carrot, spinach, and plain pasta that would be contrasted with peanut butter beige and eggplant brown. The veal would come from the best butcher shop rather than from the local supermarket. Sometimes you can tell the difference, sometimes not. This time we would go for the best possibilities our minds could conjure.

Two Asian markets were needed because of the diverse number of vegetables, spices, and herbs to be used. In the Thai market we were able to get the fresh mint leaves, curry, and cilantro. From the Korean, the vegetables, basil, and jalapeño peppers.

We also chose these markets in order to expose ourselves to something sweet and unusual that might stimulate some ideas for a dessert. What we found was fresh ginger, the sight of beautifully stacked coconuts from the Pacific, and Chinese lychees. They eventually grew into what would be called Merinque Surprise . . . or . . . perhaps Baked Ginger Mousse Bombe . . . or . . .

LUCILLE: "What should we do for the crust?"

CLAIRE: "I always like chocolate for dessert."

LUCILLE: "In the crust? I really don't like chocolate."

CLAIRE: "Okay. Let's do a graham cracker crust in a spring form pan, but I know I'm going to want chocolate somewhere."

LUCILLE: "Then how about mixing in almonds, fresh ginger, and chocolate slivers."

CLAIRE: "Now what's the next layer? It has to be striking."

LUCILLE: "Frozen yogurt!"

CLAIRE: "Not if we want to have cake layers and serve it at room temperature."

LUCILLE: "Okay, mousse—ginger mousse, and then we can mix it with fruit—mangos, blueberries, and kiwi; something that'll give a sharp contrast to the mousse."

CLAIRE: "Now that's interesting! Makes me laugh, ginger mousse. But then let's take the ginger out of the crust. Too much. I think it needs a layer of chocolate cake somewhere."

LUCILLE: "Okay. A layer of rich chocolate cake between the mousse and the crust."

CLAIRE: "The crisp crust on the bottom and the layer of chocolate cake next. That'll give a cushion for the ginger mousse to rest upon."

LUCILLE: "Then let's take the fruit out of the mousse and make the fruit a separate layer—it will be the floor for the mousse."

CLAIRE: "I like it: the frame, the cushion, the hardwood floor, and the mousse. We know it would look nice if it were a house. Let's hope it tastes good."

LUCILLE: "But we need something more—on top of the mousse . . . another layer of fruit. What about grapes?"

CLAIRE: "You're really serious about another layer aren't you? Okay. Okay. Let me think . . . how about those little, delicate champagne grapes."

LUCILLE: "No way. Those skins leave your tongue dry at times. Maybe we should have slices of Asian pears."

We had tentatively decided on a layer of sliced peaches on top of the mousse when, from out of left field, Lucille confessed her desire to do a Baked Alaska. Claire threw up her hands in exasperation: "We'll put a layer of meringue on top and call it Baked California. Will that satisfy you!?!"

Would the laws of gravity uphold such an edifice? The only way to know whether it would all work would be to try to make it.

We began making the cake two days before the dinner party. It was the most experimental food item on the menu, and we knew we would be disagreeing as much about the preparation as we had about the menu selections.

Much to Claire's dismay, Lucille's enthusiasm produced a new idea for the crust that eliminated the original call for graham cracker, replacing it with vanilla wafers. But much to Claire's surprise, the crust worked.

On the other hand, the layer of chocolate cake turned out to be too heavy. They would need to add egg whites to lighten the texture. The layers of fruit were too thin, lacking a distinctive bite and strong flavor. But the meringue turned out just right. These problems lent themselves to tinkering, but they had given themselves plenty of time to refine and redo.

But the big surprise was the ginger mousse. At first something seemed wrong. Claire folded the freshly grated ginger into lightly beaten, whipped cream, but while attempting to increase the thickness and volume, she noticed that the mixture was turning into liquid. Assuming that the problem was in the cream, she made the journey back to the store, and this time decided to whip the cream to a much stiffer state before putting in the ginger. The whipped cream thickened, she added the ginger, and the mixture immediately liquefied. It might have taken a chemist to tell us what kind of new compound we had created, but it didn't take anyone else to tell us that this "ginger river" would not substitute for ginger mousse. The "oh my!" we hoped for had turned into an "oh no!"

Then inspiration struck, and we decided to create a custard-like filling using dried ground ginger. Throwing the whipped cream and caution to the wind, we didn't even call a chemist. We would take our chances, as would our guests.

A few hours later, the bottom crust and the cake were completed. All layers would remain separated until the afternoon before the meal. With happy and somewhat pompous grins, we felt fulfilled.

THE DAY BEFORE

The items to be prepared: potatoes for the ramekin crust, the seafood curry, tarragon dressing, the barbecue sauce, the spinach washed, the salad ingredients cut, peanut butter sauce, pureed cranberry sauce for the mangos, veal rollettes made ready for the oven the following day.

We had taken on quite a day's work. Five hours if all went well, all day if the unanticipated should come to pass. Remaining true to form, Lucille's attitude was that of blissful, naive anticipation. At one point, like a child at play, she said, "I've been looking forward to this. It's like playing in a sandbox all day." Equally true to form was Claire's somewhat different attitude, aptly expressed in her response, "Yeah, well let's hope this dinner turns out to be more than just building castles in the sand!"

After a day of successes, failures, and detours, ultimately everything fell into place. The curry seafood needed the addition of plain yogurt to the coconut milk for more liquid. The mint leaves would not puree for the mango slices, requiring a change in the recipe and a trip to the supermarket. The original salad called for different kinds of peppers and mushrooms, but peppers were being used in the sauce for the entree and mushrooms were to be barbecued on the skewers. So we opted for cherry tomatoes and olives instead and, alas, another trip to the market. The sun had set and the children-at-play were up well beyond bedtime before all was set for D-Day.

D(INNER)-DAY

Plan of Action: No need for a clock. Anticipation is today's alarm.

Combine the salad ingredients first and place in an air-tight container in the refrigerator. Spinach rolls to be made and refrigerated. Veal rollettes constructed. The mango dish would follow and be refrigerated. All of these would keep until serving time.

The curried seafood ramekins would be constructed, refrigerated, and taken out 1 hour before baking time. With all of that completed by noon, it was now time for the barbecued vegetables to be cut and skewered. They would ultimately need about 15 minutes on the electric barbecue.

What remained would have to be done just before or during dinner: heating the ramekins, making the pasta, cooking the veal rollettes, and putting the meringue layer on the cake and baking it.

With a sigh of relief that spoke of everything coming together on schedule, we set the table. Faces made up and bodies dressed, the eight-o'clock hour approached. So too did stage fright, melancholia, wistful philosophizing, nervous laughter, and the realization that after days of preparation and a few hours of actual consumption, what we ultimately will have created is a memory for ourselves and our family and friends.

THE RECIPES FOR DINNER AT EIGHT

CURRY SEAFOOD RAMEKINS

- 8   *small ceramic ramekins and 1 pastry bag fitted with decorative tip*
- 8   *large shrimp, peeled and deveined*
- 8   *large scallops*
- ¾   *pound fresh firm-fleshed fish (shark, seabass, swordfish) cut in small pieces*
- 5   *large baking potatoes*
- ½   *cup heavy cream*
- ¼   *cup butter*
- ½   *cup yogurt*
-     *salt and pepper to taste*
- 6   *ounces grated Parmesan cheese and 2 tablespoons extra for topping*

CURRY SAUCE

- ½2   *onion, diced*
- 2   *tablespoons peanut or canola oil*
- 2   *cloves fresh garlic, pressed*
- 1   *tablespoon chili powder*
- 1   *teaspoon cumin*
- 1   *teaspoon ground coriander*
- 1   *teaspoon tumeric*
- 1   *teaspoon cardamon*
- 1   *teaspoon ginger*
- 1   *teaspoon ground black peppercorns*
- ½   *teaspoon cayenne pepper*
- 1   *teaspoon salt*
- 1   *cup coconut milk*

To prepare Curry Sauce: in a small frying pan, sauté the onion in 1 tablespoon of oil until golden. Add the rest of the Curry Sauce ingredients and cook 2 to 3 minutes. Add the coconut milk slowly to form a thick sauce.

———

Put all fish, shrimp, and scallops in a steamer and steam 3 to 4 minutes. Remove from steamer and let cool. Cut the fish, shrimp, and scallops into bite-size pieces. Add to the curry sauce and mix well. Set aside.

To prepare Potato Crust: boil the potatoes approximately 40 minutes in a large pot of salted water. Remove the skins. In a large bowl, put the potatoes, grated cheese, cream, butter, and yogurt and blend until creamy. Add salt and pepper to taste.

Divide the seafood mixture into the ramekins. Fill the pastry bag with the potato mixture and make a crust to cover the seafood. Sprinkle with 2 extra tablespoons of cheese. Set aside.

Bake at 350° for 15 minutes. Then put under the broiler until potatoes are brown, approximately 2 minutes.

SPINACH ROLLS

serves 8

2	*large bunches of fresh spinach*
	a small pinch of nutmeg
½	*cup toasted sesame seeds*
1 to 3	*tablespoons tamari or soy sauce*
	salt and pepper to taste
2	*whole scallions*

Wash the spinach thoroughly. Remove the stems. Layer the spinach leaves in a steamer, seasoning each layer with a touch of nutmeg. Steam until just wilted.

Place the spinach and tamari into a bowl and mix well. Squeeze out excess tamari. Salt and pepper to taste.

With your hands, divide the spinach leaves into eight sections and sprinkle each section with sesame seeds. Roll up each section, cigar style.

Remove the bulb from each scallion and cut each green stem into thin, ribbon-like slivers. Wrap the slivers around the spinach rolls and tie in a knot. Refrigerate until well chilled.

PEANUT BUTTER PASTA WITH BARBECUED EGGPLANT AND SKEWERED BARBECUED VEGETABLES TO BE SERVED WITH VEAL

3	small Japanese eggplants
	salt
12	large mushrooms
8	small boiling onions
2	red and/or green peppers
3	large zucchinis
½	cup peanut butter sauce (see page 82 for recipe)
1½	pounds fresh fettuccini, cooked and drained

BARBECUE SAUCE

½	cup olive oil
3	cloves garlic, minced
3	tablespoons chili powder
¼	cup fresh basil, chopped
1	teaspoon dried oregano
3	teaspoons Worcestershire sauce

Heat the grill

In a bowl, combine all the ingredients for the barbecue sauce, then set aside.

Slice the eggplants and lightly salt them. Let them rest for 30 minutes. Rinse. Pat dry. Cut the remaining vegetables in large chunks and brush with barbecue sauce. Skewer all the vegetables except the eggplant slices, which go directly on the grill. Baste regularly to avoid burning.

Toss the peanut butter sauce into the pasta and decorate with the eggplant slices. Serve the vegetables on skewers.

MANGO SLICES WITH VANILLA YOGURT AND CRANBERRY PUREE

serves 8

½   *can whole cranberries*
2   *tablespoons lime juice*
½   *cup vanilla yogurt*
2   *very large, ripe mangos, chilled, sliced thin*
8   *mint leaves*

Puree the cranberries with the lime juice. Puree the yogurt separately.

Fill one small plastic squirt bottle (with a pointed tip; available at beauty supply stores or drug stores) with the cranberry puree. Using the tip as a pen, draw a ring of cranberries on each chilled dessert plate. Using a second bottle, do the same with the yogurt, right inside the cranberry ring. Then take a toothpick and, with a zig-zag motion, merge one circle within the other.

Place 3 slices of mango on each plate. Place 2 mint leaves and a cranberry connecting their stems on the middle of the mango slices.

VEAL ROLLETTE WITH ROASTED PEPPER SAUCE

serves 8

1	*pound chopped veal*
¼	*cup chopped Italian flat parsley*
½	*cup grated Asiago cheese*
¼	*cup grated carrots*
½	*cup bread crumbs*
½	*cup pignoli nuts, toasted*
1	*egg*
2½	*teaspoons salt*
2	*large poblano peppers, roasted and skin removed**
1	*large green pepper*
1	*bunch cilantro*
2	*cloves garlic, crushed*
2	*tablespoons olive oil*
8	*veal scallops*

Veal Filling: in a bowl, combine the chopped veal, parsley, cheese, carrots, bread crumbs, pignoli nuts, egg, and 1½ teaspoons of salt. Mix well and set aside.

Rollette Sauce: in a blender, combine the roasted bell peppers, cilantro, garlic, olive oil, and 1 teaspoon salt. Puree and set aside.

To make the Rollette: preheat the oven to 350°.

Put the veal scallops between sheets of wax paper and gently pound each one to approximately ¼-inch thick.

Overlap the veal scallops to form an approximately 9 × 13-inch slab. Spoon the veal filling over the entire slab up to 1 inch from the edge. Roll

---

*To roast the peppers, place seeded halved peppers, skin side up, on greased baking dish. Broil under high heat until the skins turn black. Place in a paper bag for 10 minutes. Remove, peel, and chop.

the slab up into a jelly roll and secure with kitchen string. Place the rollette into a greased baking dish and brush sauce over the entire roll, leaving some for basting and place the roll into the oven for 45 to 60 minutes, basting every 15 minutes.

When done, let stand for 5 minutes before slicing. Serve with remaining sauce.

THE UNEXPECTED SALAD

serves 8

1	*head red leaf lettuce*
½	*head romaine lettuce*
¼	*pound radish sprouts*
1	*cucumber, peeled and seeded*
4	*scallions*
1	*cup kalamata pitted olives*
20	*cherry tomatoes, cut in half*

Clean and tear lettuce. Cut the scallions, tomatoes, and cucumbers. Combine all the ingredients in large bowl.

CREAMY TARRAGON DRESSING

2	*tablespoons mayonnaise*
¼	*cup olive oil*
¼	*cup peanut oil*
1	*bunch fresh tarragon*
⅓	*cup rice vinegar*
6	*cloves garlic, mashed*
1	*tablespoon Dijon mustard*
1	*tablespoon fresh black pepper*
	salt to taste

Put all the ingredients in the blender and mix until smooth and creamy. Refrigerate.

THE SECOND TIME AROUND
MOUSSE BOMBE

serves 8 to 10

FIRST LAYER—CRUST

- 6 ounces toasted almonds
- 6 tablespoons hard butter
- 1 tablespoon vanilla
  pinch of salt
- 1 tablespoon honey
- 10 vanilla wafers
- 2 ounces bittersweet chocolate chips

Place all the ingredients in a Cuisinart and blend until the mixture resembles coarse meal. Set aside.

SECOND AND FOURTH LAYER—CHOCOLATE CAKE

- 3 ounces unsweetened baking chocolate
- ¾ cup sugar
- ¾ cup buttermilk
- ¾ cup sifted cake flour
- 1 teaspoon baking powder
- 1 teaspoon baking soda
- 1 teaspoon salt
- ⅓ cup butter
- 3 eggs
- 1 teaspoon vanilla

Preheat oven to 350°. Melt the chocolate in a saucepan over low heat, stirring until smooth. Add ¼ cup sugar and ¼ cup buttermilk and blend. Let cool. Mix the flour, baking powder, soda, and salt. Cream the butter.

Gradually beat the remaining ½ cup sugar into the butter. Add the eggs one at a time, thoroughly mixing each into the batter. Blend in ½ of the flour mixture, all of the chocolate mixture, and the vanilla and beat. Add the rest of the flour mixture and ½ cup of buttermilk. Beat until smooth. Pour into a greased and floured 9-inch spring form pan. Bake at 350° for 40 minutes or until a toothpick inserted in the middle comes out clean. Let cool. Remove from pan and slice in half horizontally.

THIRD AND FIFTH LAYER— GINGER CUSTARD (PREPARE 1 DAY AHEAD)

¾	*envelope of unflavored gelatin*
1½	*tablespoons cold water*
2	*eggs, separated*
½	*cup plus 1 tablespoon sugar*
1	*tablespoon cornstarch*
1½	*cups milk*
2	*tablespoons powdered ginger (do not use fresh ginger)*
	pinch of salt
1	*pint whipping cream, beaten until stiff*
2	*teaspoons vanilla*

Soften the gelatin in the cold water and set aside.

Beat the egg yolks slowly and add ½ cup sugar until thick and creamy. Add the cornstarch and blend well. Add gelatin mixture.

Gradually add the milk to the egg mixture. Pour into a heavy enamel pot. Over low flame, cook until the mixture thickens without boiling. Stir in the ginger and vanilla and set aside.

Beat the egg whites with the remaining tablespoon of sugar and the salt until stiff and glossy, fold into the custard mix.

When the mixture cools, fold in the whipped cream. Cover the mixture and refrigerate overnight.

SIXTH LAYER

    1   *pint of fresh strawberries, sliced*

SEVENTH LAYER—MERINGUE DOME

    6   *tablespoons sugar*
    ½   *teaspoon salt*
    ½   *teaspoon cream of tartar*
    6   *egg whites*

Prepare immediately before serving.

Preheat the oven to 450°.

Beat the egg whites with the salt in a grease free bowl and cream of tartar until very light and foamy. Slowly add the sugar, 1 tablespoon at a time until meringue forms stiff, glossy peaks.

CAKE ASSEMBLY INSTRUCTIONS

1. Press the first layer, the crust, on the bottom of a spring-form pan.

2. Arrange the second layer, the chocolate cake, on top of the first layer.

3. Spoon half of the third layer, the ginger custard, on top of the second layer.

4. Arrange the second layer of chocolate cake on top of the third layer.

5. Spoon the remaining half of the ginger custard on top of the fourth layer.

6. Arrange sixth layer, strawberries, on top of the fifth layer.

Remove the side of the spring-form pan and cover the entire cake with meringue, sealing the bottom well. Bake at 450° for 4 to 5 minutes or until the top is lightly browned. Serve immediately or refrigerate.

CHAPTER TEN

THE LASAGNA POSTSCRIPT

"The only joy in the world is to begin."

—CESARE PAVESE

AFTER THE MEAL, WHICH PROVED TO BE A CREATIVE SUCCESS, WE ASKED OUR guests, in the spirit of the Zen of cooking, to help create some lasagna recipes. The following recipe was given out, and the guests were asked to change the electives for an original twist. Free to roam the kitchen and cupboards looking for new ideas, the abounding enthusiasm produced some inventive recipes. All recipes serve 4 to 6.

LASAGNA

1	16-ounce box lasagna noodles
2	tablespoons olive oil
½	onion, finely chopped
1	pound ground turkey
2	cloves garlic, minced
	salt to taste
⅛	teaspoon cayenne pepper
2	teaspoons savory
2	tablespoons chopped parsley
16	ounces ricotta cheese
1	pound mozzarella cheese, grated
2	cups homemade or jarred tomato sauce
½	cup grated Parmesan cheese

Preheat oven to 370°.

Prepare the lasagna noodles according to the package directions. In a heavy skillet, heat the oil and sauté the onions for 5 minutes. Add the turkey, garlic, salt, cayenne, and savory and stir until the meat is separated into small pieces—about 7 minutes. Remove from heat.

In a bowl, mix the parsley into the ricotta cheese. Place a layer of noodles on the bottom of a greased 9 × 12-inch pan. Spread half of the ricotta mixture, half of the turkey mixture, half of the grated mozzarella, and half of the tomato sauce over the noodles. Repeat. Sprinkle the top with Parmesan cheese.

Bake 25 to 30 minutes. Let stand 10 minutes and serve.

THE ORIGINAL RECIPES

SPINACH LASAGNA

serves 6 - 8

1	*16-ounce box lasagna noodles*
2	*10-ounce packages frozen spinach, defrosted; squeeze juice out through a 12-inch square cheese cloth*
1	*bunch scallions, chopped*
1	*bunch fresh basil, stems removed*
8	*cloves fresh garlic, cut in half*
2	*tablespoons olive oil*
3	*tablespoons soy sauce*
16	*ounces low-fat ricotta cheese*
½	*cup grated Reggiano cheese*
1	*pound grated mozzarella cheese*
2	*cups homemade or jarred tomato sauce*

Preheat the oven to 375°.

Sauté the spinach, scallions, basil, and garlic in olive oil until tender. Transfer to a food processor. Add the soy sauce and ricotta cheese and blend.

Prepare the noodles according to the package directions. Place a layer of noodles on the bottom of a greased 13 × 9 × 2-inch pan. Spread a layer of Reggiano cheese, then the spinach mixture, then the mozzarella and some sauce. Repeat. Place a layer of noodles on the top and cover with tomato sauce and the remaining cheeses.

Place the pan on the uppermost rack of the oven and bake for 25 to 30 minutes, until the top forms a golden crust. Allow to settle 10 minutes before serving.

TAMALE PIE LASAGNA

MEAT FILLING

1	*16-ounce box lasagna noodles*
1½	*pounds lean ground turkey*
1	*large onion, chopped*
¼	*cup chopped raisins*
½	*cup chopped roasted peppers*
2	*tablespoons capers*
1	*teaspoon honey*
1	*cup beef stock*
2	*tablespoons chili powder*
¼	*teaspoon cayenne pepper*
2	*teaspoons salt*

TAMALE TOPPING

¾	*cup cornmeal*
1	*tablespoon flour*
1	*teaspoon salt*
½	*teaspoon baking powder*
1	*egg, slightly beaten*
¼	*cup chopped mild canned green chilis*
⅓	*cup milk*
1	*tablespoon olive oil*
6	*ounces Parmesan cheese*

Preheat the oven to 350°.

To roast the peppers, place seeded halved peppers, skin side up, on a greased baking dish. Broil under high heat until the skins turn black. Place in a paper bag for 10 minutes. Remove, peel, and chop.

In a skillet, brown the turkey. Add the remaining Meat Filling ingredients. Cover and simmer for 15 minutes. Uncover and simmer for 5 minutes. Set aside.

In a bowl, add all the Tamale Topping ingredients and mix well.

Prepare noodles according to the package directions. Place a layer of noodles in a greased 13 × 9 × 2-inch pan. Add a layer of meat and a layer of tamale. Repeat. Place a layer of noodles on top and cover with Parmesan cheese. Bake at 350° for 25 minutes. Let stand 10 minutes.

VEGETABLE QUICHE LASAGNA

1   *16-ounce box lasagna noodles*

1   *large eggplant or 5 Japanese eggplants halved, stems and tips removed*

3   *red peppers, cut in half and seeded*

5   *zucchinis, ends removed*

2   *cups tomato sauce*

1   *cup milk*

3   *eggs*

1   *teaspoon ground rosemary*

1   *teaspoon basil*

½   *onion, thinly sliced*

1   *cup grated provolone cheese*

½   *cup grated white cheddar cheese*

½   *cup grated Parmesan cheese*

Preheat the oven to 350°.

Steam the eggplant, peppers, and zucchini until tender. Remove and slice. Let stand until cool and the water is drained.

With a wire whisk, mix the tomato sauce, milk, eggs, rosemary, and basil until frothy.

Cook pasta according to package directions.

Place a layer of pasta on the bottom of a greased 13 × 9 × 2-inch pan. Place half of the vegetables and the sliced onion on the pasta, sprinkle with half of the provolone and half of the cheddar cheese. Pour in half of the tomato sauce mixture. Repeat. Finish with a layer of pasta, and sprinkle with Parmesan cheese.

Bake for 40 minutes. Let stand 10 minutes.

MEXICAN LASAGNA

1   *16-ounce box lasagna noodles*
2   *pounds ground beef*
1   *onion, finely chopped*
2   *celery stalks, finely chopped*
1   *red pepper, finely chopped*
1   *tablespoon hot chili powder*
½   *cup chopped fresh cilantro*
1   *16-ounce can refried beans, no lard*
8   *ounces grated white cheddar cheese*
8   *ounces grated mozzarella cheese*
1   *8-ounce can green taco sauce*
1   *tablespoon oil*

Preheat the oven to 350°.

Prepare the pasta according to the package instructions.

Brown the beef in a skillet in 1 tablespoon oil and remove the fat. Add the onion, celery, pepper, and chili powder and cook for 10 minutes or until vegetables are tender. Stir in the cilantro.

Place a layer of pasta on the bottom of a greased 13 × 9 × 2-inch pan. Cover with half of the refried beans and half of the meat and sprinkle with 3 ounces of cheddar and 3 ounces mozzarella cheese. Add another layer of pasta, spread with half of the refried beans, 3 ounces of mozzarella, and 3 ounces of cheddar cheese. Place a layer of pasta on top and cover with 2 ounces of mozzarella and 2 ounces of cheddar cheese. Pour on the taco sauce, pushing it around the sides. Bake for 35 minutes. Let stand 10 minutes.

RED HOT HERBED LASAGNA

1	16-ounce lasagna noodes
1	large onion, chopped
1½	pounds mushrooms, sliced
3	zucchini, thinly sliced
2	tablespoons sweet paprika
2	teaspoons red chili flakes
2	teaspoons cumin
5	garlic cloves, crushed
1	teaspoon allspice
2	teaspoons rosemary, crushed
3	tablespoons vegetable oil
2	tablespoons soy sauce
1	tablespoon white wine
2½	cups ricotta cheese
16	ounces mozzarella cheese, grated
2	cups tomato sauce

Preheat the oven to 350°.

Sauté the onions, mushrooms, zucchini, paprika, chili flakes, cumin, garlic, allspice, and rosemary in the vegetable oil until onions are clear. Add the soy sauce and white wine and simmer for 1 minute. Let the pan cool. Stir in the ricotta cheese.

Cook pasta according to package directions.

Place one layer of pasta on bottom of a greased 13 × 9 × 2-inch pan. Overlap with half of the ricotta mixture, then ⅓ of the mozzarella cheese, and ⅓ of the sauce. Repeat. Cover the top with a layer of noodles and ⅓ of the mozzarella cheese and ⅓ of the sauce. Bake 45 minutes. Let stand 10 minutes and serve.

FRUITS DE MER LASAGNA

1   *16-ounce box lasagna noodles*
½   *pound salmon, cut into small pieces*
½   *pound halibut, cut into small pieces*
½   *pound red snapper, cut into small pieces*
½   *pound mushrooms, sliced*
4   *tablespoons fresh tarragon or 2 tablespoons dried*
3   *tablespoons vegetable oil*
2   *large carrots, sliced or grated*
1   *pound broccoli, cut into small flowerettes*
     16-ounce box lasagna noodles
4   *tablespoons Peccorino, Romano or Parmesan cheese grated*
½   *teaspoon cayenne pepper*

BÉCHAMEL SAUCE

5   *tablespoons butter*
4½   *tablespoons flour*
1   *cup grated Parmesan cheese*
⅛   *teaspoon grated nutmeg*
     pinch salt
3   *cups milk*

Preheat the oven to 350°.

Cook pasta according to package directions.

Sauté the fish, mushrooms, cayenne pepper, and tarragon in 1 tablespoon of vegetable oil until the fish is just about cooked. Set aside. Sauté the carrots in 1 tablespoon of vegetable oil until slightly soft. Parboil the broccoli, then sauté in 1 tablespoon of vegetable oil until tender.

Make Béchamel Sauce: melt the butter over low heat. Whisk in the flour, Parmesan cheese, nutmeg, and salt. Heat the milk to a low simmer. Slowly pour the milk into the flour mixture, whisking well. Turn off the heat.

Place a layer of pasta on the bottom of a greased 13 × 9 × 2-inch pan. Cover with the fish mixture. Pour ¼ of the béchamel over that. Cover with a pasta layer. Cover with the carrot mixture and ¼ of the béchamel. Add another layer of pasta, then the broccoli layer, and ½ of the béchamel. Top with a layer of pasta and the rest of the béchamel and the Peccorino cheese. Bake for 35 minutes. Let stand 10 minutes and serve.

INDEX